PEACE KILLS

P. J. O'ROURKE is the bestselling author of ten books, including *Eat the Rich*, *Give War a Chance*, *Holidays in Hell*, *Parliament of Whores*, *All the Trouble in the World* and *The CEO of the Sofa*. He has contributed to, among other publications, *Playboy*, *Esquire*, *Harper's*, *New Republic*, the *New York Times Book Review* and *Vanity Fair*. He is a regular correspondent for the *Atlantic* magazine. He divides his time between New Hampshire and Washington, DC.

ALSO BY P. J. O'ROURKE

Modern Manners

The Bachelor Home Companion

Republican Party Reptile

Holidays in Hell

Parliament of Whores

Give War a Chance

All the Trouble in the World

Age and Guile

Eat the Rich

P. J. O'ROURKE

PEACE
KILLS

PICADOR

First published 2004 by Atlantic Monthly Press,
an imprint of Grove Atlantic, Inc., New York

First published in Great Britain 2004 by Atlantic Books, an imprint of Grove Atlantic Ltd

First published in paperback 2005 by Picador
an imprint of Pan Macmillan Ltd
Pan Macmillan, 20 New Wharf Road, London N1 9RR
Basingstoke and Oxford
Associated companies throughout the world
www.panmacmillan.com

ISBN 0 330 43781 X

1 3 5 7 9 8 6 4 2

A CIP catalogue record for this book is available from
the British Library.

Printed and bound in Great Britain by
Mackays of Chatham plc, Chatham, Kent

In Memory of Michael Kelly

He could have advocated the war in Iraq without going to cover it. He could have covered it without putting himself in harm's way. But liberty is an expensive feast. And Mike was a man who always picked up the check.

CONTENTS

1 WHY AMERICANS HATE FOREIGN POLICY   1

2 KOSOVO   17
November 1999

3 ISRAEL   31
April 2001

4 9/11 DIARY   57

5 EGYPT   81
December 2001

6 NOBEL SENTIMENTS   115

7 WASHINGTON, D.C., DEMONSTRATIONS   123
April 2002

8 THOUGHTS ON THE EVE OF WAR   139

9 KUWAIT AND IRAQ   143
March and April 2003

10 POSTSCRIPT: IWO JIMA AND THE END OF   187
MODERN WARFARE
July 2003

ACKNOWLEDGMENTS

I like the places I write about. I enjoy the people. I've had a good time wherever I've gone, Iraq included. My subject, in a way, is pleasure. This is really a book about pleasantness, which is why I dedicate it to Mike Kelly. He and I were drinking one night—a pleasurable occasion—and I remember him saying, "Wouldn't it be *pleasant* if we could do something with the forces of evil other than hunt them down and kill them?" If we increased funding and reduced class sizes at the fundamentalist *madras* schools . . . If all the Mrs. bin Ladens had access to day care and prenatal health services . . . If, when Germanic hordes were threatening Rome, a Security Council meeting of the United Despotisms had been called, and Marcus Aurelius had pursued a multilateral foreign policy working in cooperation with the Parthians, the Huns, and the

Han Chinese . . . If Aztec priests had taken it on faith that their captives had a lot of heart . . . If Australopithecus and the saber-toothed tiger had engaged in meaningful dialogue . . .

> How pleasing would the whole world be,
> If everyone would just say please.

And thank you, too, of course, thanks being what this part of a book is about. I thank Mike Kelly—a little late, as heart-felt thanks tend to be. But I assume that Mike is keeping current in Reporters' Heaven (open bar and porthole in the floor through which highly placed sources quoted on the condition of anonymity can be watched as they fry). A few years back Mike took over as editor of *The Atlantic*. I was writing for *Rolling Stone*, where my job was to be the Republican. After sixteen years even *Rolling Stone* had figured out that this made as much sense as offering readers a free bris. Also my excellent and long-suffering editor there, Bob Love, was about to head to someplace where "Marcus Aurelius" would not be mistaken for Beyoncé's latest brand of bling. Mike called and said, "I can pay you less."

Most of this book originally appeared, in somewhat different form, in *The Atlantic*, first under the brilliant editorship of Mike Kelly, then under the brilliant editorship of Cullen Murphy. If you think the book good, behold what three short Irishmen can accomplish when they've lost the key to the liquor cabinet. If you think the book otherwise, assume that, after a certain amount of feeling around in the carpet, they found it.

The first chapter contains material from a piece that appeared in *The Wall Street Journal*, on the op-ed page edited by

Max Boot—may he long give enemies of America a taste of his name.

I'm not sure that Bob Love would care to do that to Robert Bork. But it was under Love's stewardship of *Rolling Stone* that "Kosovo—November 1999" appeared with its Borkian pessimism, doubtless causing a puzzled tug of a lip ring and a quick flip of the page by more than one reader. As important as getting "Kosovo" into print was getting there in the first place. Irena Ivanova and Biljana Bosiljanova of the Macedonian Press Center made all the arrangements. Nothing has ever been simple or easy in the Balkans except for my stay there, thanks to Irena and Biljana.

My old friend Dave Garcia came from Hong Kong to travel with me through both Israel and Egypt, just for the hell of it. (Luckily, no literal experience of the cliché was had.) Dave has a knack for finding tequila in the least likely places. Besides being good company, he is universally *simpatico*. The most foreign foreigners take to Dave immediately. He understands their point of view. It is Dave's opinion that everybody's point of view can be understood if you stipulate that everybody is crazy. When it comes to intelligent treatment of foreigners, Dave is the next best thing to Thorazine.

Not that it was always the foreigners who needed the psychiatric aid. Talking to Ashraf Kalil was therapeutic in helping me cope with that maddening city Cairo. Michele Lieber was a link to sanity on 9/11/01, as was the Palm restaurant in Washington, D.C., where I've been taking medication for years under the supervision of Tommy Jacomo, Jocelyn Zarr, and Kevin Rudowski. And, during the initial weeks of the Iraq war, I would have gone nuts from boredom if I hadn't had excellent companions with whom to crawl the walls of Kuwait. Chief among these were Matt Labash and Steve Hayes of *The Weekly Standard* and the "room boy" at their hotel. The last shall go unnamed, but if any reader is offered the chance to direct a remake of *Thunder Road* set in Kuwait, please cast that young fellow in the Robert Mitchum moonshine-running hero role.

Alas, most of the time in Kuwait was passed sober, and there wasn't much to do but pass the time. Long conversations with pals when neither you nor they have had a drink can be a test of palship. I fear I received an "Incomplete." Others passed with honors: Alex Travelli of ABC, Simon McCoy and Philip Chadwick of Sky News, Cohn Baker of ITN, Ernie Alexander, Marco Sotos, Spanish documentary filmmaker Esteban Uyarra, and my friends Charlie Glass and Sal Aridi, whom I met at my virgin war, in Lebanon, twenty years ago.

ABC News, as it has many times before, allowed me into its Big Top and let me tag along with the parade of real journalists. I suppose they hope that one day I'll grab a shovel and clean up behind the elephants. In lieu of that, they gave me a part-time job as the world's worst radio reporter. ("This is P. J. O'Rourke in Kuwait City and not a darn thing is happening.") My boss in Kuwait, Vic Ratner—a real radio reporter with the old-school voice and the AK-47 delivery—was more than welcoming and patient. Thank you, Vic, and thank you, Chris Isham, Burt Rudman, Peter Jennings, John Meyerson, Deirdre Michalopoulos, Wayne Fisk, John Quinones, and all the cameramen, soundmen, and technicians in whose way I constantly was. Here's to you, ABC News—don't let them make you wear those mouse ears on camera.

Thanks also to Alex Vogel, who did his best to repair a faltering ABC Land Rover in Iraq by phone from New Hampshire. Looting was rife in Iraq at the time and Alex asked—amid discussion of diesel compression loss due to piston scoring from desert grit—"If New York is ever freed from oppression by liberals, will there be looting in Manhattan?" I believe, Alex, that Manhattanites have been doing that all along, on Wall Street. But there *will* be plenty of sniping from *The New York Review of Books.*

Max Blumenfeld, from the Department of Defense, managed to get me to Baghdad, where Major William Dean Thurmond made me at home. Dean, you are an officer, a gentleman, and damn handy at making coffee in plastic sacks using the chemical heater packs from the Meals Ready to Eat. Additional thanks to Major Mike Birmingham, of the Third Infantry Division, and a tip o' the pants to Derek and Ski (they'll know what I mean).

At the Baghdad airport I was billeted with good friends of mine, the courageous and beautiful Alisha Ryu from Voice of America and the equally courageous if not quite so good-looking Steve Kamarow of *USA Today.* With us was *The Phila-delphia Inquirer*'s Andrea Gerlin, fresh from combat coverage with a brilliant idea for selling American women a fitness and weight-loss program based on sleeping in holes, getting shot at, and eating MREs. James Kitfield from *The Atlantic*'s sister publication, *The National Journal,* was there as well. Kitfield is fluent in the language of the military, which is harder to translate than Arabic. Were it not for James, I would still be pondering what it means to be in a part of town that was "controlled but not secured" and thus I would be blown to bits.

We had, as I mentioned, a good time in Baghdad. Chaos is interesting. Reporters would rather be interested than comfortable. Put that way, it sounds noble enough. Put another way, we would rather be interested than well paid, worthwhile, responsible, or smart.

Fifty-nine years ago Iwo Jima might have been a little *too* interesting for this reporter. At least it's still uncomfortable. It was the idea of Tim Baney to take me to Iwo. Please use Baney Media Incorporated for all your television programming needs. (Except Tim doesn't do weddings, although for a price . . .) We traveled with ace cameraman Pat Anderson—three Irishmen again, but this time only one of us was short. Transport from Okinawa was arranged through the kind offices of Kim Newberry and Captain Chris Perrine, USMC. On the island battlefield we were entertained (if that verb ever can be used in connection with war) and instructed (a verb not used in connection with war often enough) by Sergeant Major Mike McClure, USMC, and Sergeant Major Suwa, Japanese Self-Defense Forces.

There are many other people to whom I owe thanks. My thanks credit is woefully overextended. I am in gratitude Chapter 11. Any number of debts of obligation doubtless will go unpaid as I attempt to settle my accounts. For years Max Pappas was my invaluable research assistant. I know he misses sitting in the kitchen trying to extract *Dora the Explorer* from the disk drive while dog and children gnaw on his pants cuffs. And I'm sure he's much less happy and fulfilled in his present position as policy analyst at Citizens for a Sound Economy, no matter what he says to the contrary.

Likewise, sisters Caitlin and Megan Rhodes escaped the same kitchen computer post to, respectively, go to college and pursue a career in Chicago. They are probably, this minute, sprinkling dog hair and Froot Loops onto their laptop keyboards for nostalgia's sake.

Dr. William Hughes has kept me healthy through years of Third World travel. He carefully researches the hideous diseases that rage in the places I'm about to visit, gives me a bottle of pills, and says, "Take these if you begin to bleed from the ears and maybe you'll live to be medevaced."

For all questions on military matters, I go to Lieutenant Colonel Mike Schellhammer, who introduced me to my wife and who, therefore, she tells me, cannot be wrong about anything. If there are errors about military-type things in the following pages, it's because Mike, an intelligence officer, is very tight-lipped. "I could tell you what I do," Mike says, "but I'd have to bore you to death."

Don Epstein and his colleagues at Greater Talent Network continue to find lectures for me to give and lecture audiences who do not throw things that are large or rotten.

My literary agent, Bob Dattila, maintains his remarkable ability to extract money from people in return for work that accidentally got erased in the hard drive; was lost by UPS; just needs a slight final polish; was e-mailed yesterday, honest, but the attachment probably couldn't be opened because of that computer virus that's going around; and is really, truly, completely finished in my head—and I just need to write it down.

The Atlantic is the only magazine in America with a readership and staff who are sitting, clothed, and in their right minds. Writing for *The Atlantic* is an honor I don't deserve, and you'd think Cullen Murphy would be able to tell that from my spelling, grammar, and punctuation. But when I read what I've written in *The Atlantic*, I find that it's, mirabile dictu, in good English. (Or, if the occasion warrants, as it does with mirabile dictu, it's in good Latin. The phrase is Virgil's—as if I'd know.) This is the work of *The Atlantic*'s deputy managing editors Toby Lester and Martha Spaulding, of senior editor Yvonne Rolhausen, and of staff editors Elizabeth Shelburne, Joshua Friedman, and Jessica Murphy. Bless you all, and you, David Bradley, for buying *The Atlantic* and saving it from a dusty fate in library stacks next to bundles of *Transition, New Directions,* and *The Dial,* or a fate worse than dusty, running features such as "The Most Important One or Two Books I've Ever Read" by Charlize Theron.

Historically, Grove/Atlantic, Inc., branched from *The Atlantic Monthly,* although a cutting was made and transplanted into the rich mud of the New York literary scene, which, combined with a graft to the sturdy root of Grove Press, caused this metaphor to badly need pruning. Grove/Atlantic is a great publishing house, and I would say that even if it hadn't published all my books. Grove/Atlantic chief, Morgan Entrekin, is a true aristocrat among publishers, and I would say that even if I didn't owe him money. Go buy a lot of Grove/Atlantic books, no matter what the subject, and maybe Morgan will let me off the hook for that advance on my proposed Howard Dean presidential biography. You'll be doing a favor not just to me but to every person at Grove/Atlantic. They are all true aristocrats of publishing, albeit impoverished aristocrats due to—let's be blunt—you, negligent reader, spending your money on DVDs and video games. A prostration, a curtsy, a bow, and a yank on the forelock to Charles Rue Woods, archduke of art design; Judy Hottensen, maharani of marketing; Scott Manning, prince regent of public relations; Debra Wenger, caliph of copyediting; and Michael Hornburg and Muriel Jorgensen, potentates of production. Even if this book gets remaindered, it will be a royal flush.

There is one more performer of thankless tasks to thank. Tina O'Rourke provides sage editorial advice, pays the bills, keeps the books, raises the children, runs the household . . . But there are not trees enough to make the paper to give me the space to list all the things my wife does. I will be ecologically conscious and eschew sprawl by listing, rather, the things Tina does *not* do. She doesn't stare disconsolately at a blank page all day and come home reeking of cigar smoke and snarl at the kids and drink gin. And for these, and many other things, we love you, dear.

Let me close by acknowledging the inspiration I received from that now nearly forgotten deep thinker about foreign policy issues, General Wesley Clark. Addressing an audience in Keene, New Hampshire, during the 2004 presidential primary campaign, General Clark said, "I came into the Army because I believe in public service, not because I want to kill people." How surprised Saddam Hussein would have been to see General Clark in public, coming across the Kuwait border with a napkin over his arm, carrying a tray of bratwurst and beer.

Next year we are to bring the soldiers home
For lack of money, and it is all right.
Places they guarded, or kept orderly,
Must guard themselves, and keep themselves orderly.
We want the money for ourselves at home
Instead of working. And this is all right.

It's hard to say who wanted it to happen,
But now it's been decided nobody minds.
The places are a long way off, not here,
Which is all right, and from what we hear
The soldiers there only made trouble happen.
Next year we shall be easier in our minds.

Next year we shall be living in a country
That brought its soldiers home for lack of money.
The statues will be standing in the same
Tree-muffled squares, and look nearly the same.
Our children will not know it's a different country.
All we can hope to leave them now is money.

—Philip Larkin
"Homage to a Government"
England, 1969

1

WHY AMERICANS HATE
FOREIGN POLICY

❖

I was in Berlin in November 1989, the weekend the wall opened. The Cold War was over. The ICBMs weren't going to fly. The world wouldn't melt in a fusion fireball or freeze in a nuclear winter. Everybody was happy and relieved. And me, too, although I'm not one of those children of the 1950s who was traumatized by the A-bomb. Getting under a school desk during duck-and-cover was more interesting and less scary than the part of the multiplication table that came after "times seven." Still, the notion that, at any time, the U.S.S.R. and the U.S.A. might blow up the whole world— my neighborhood included—was in the back of my mind. A little mushroom-shaped cloud marred the sunny horizon of my future as an internationally renowned junior high school football player. If *On the Beach* was for real, I'd never get tall enough to date Ava Gardner. What's more, whenever I was apprehended in youthful hijinks, Mutually Assured Destruction failed to happen before Dad got home from work. Then, in the fall of 1962, when I was fifteen, Armageddon really did seem to arrive. I made an earnest plea to my blond, freckled biology-class lab partner (for whom, worshipfully, I had undertaken all frog dissection duties). "The Cuban missile crisis," I said, "means we probably won't live long. Let's *do it* before we die." She demurred. All in all the Cold War was a bad thing.

Twenty-seven years later, wandering through previously sinister Checkpoint Charlie with beer in hand, I felt like a weight had been lifted from my shoulders. I remember thinking just those words: "I feel like a weight has been lifted . . ." A wiser person would have been thinking, "I feel like I took a big dump."

Nastiness was already reaccumulating. I reported on some of it in ex-Soviet Georgia, ex-Yugoslav Yugoslavia, the West Bank, Somalia, and Iraq-ravaged Kuwait. The relatively simple, if costive, process of digesting the Communist bloc was complete. America needed to reconstitute its foreign policy with—so to speak—a proper balance of fruit and fiber. The serious people who ponder these things seriously said the new American foreign policy must include:

- Nation-building;
- A different approach to national security;
- Universal tenets of democracy.

This didn't occur to me. Frankly, nothing concerning foreign policy had ever occurred to me. I'd been writing about foreign countries and foreign affairs and foreigners for years. But you can own dogs all your life and not have "dog policy."

You have rules, yes—Get off the couch!—and training, sure. We want the dumb creatures to be well behaved and friendly. So we feed foreigners, take care of them, give them treats, and, when absolutely necessary, whack them with a rolled-up newspaper. That was as far as my foreign policy thinking went until the middle 1990s, when I realized America's foreign policy thinking hadn't gone that far.

In the fall of 1996, I traveled to Bosnia to visit a friend whom I'll call Major Tom. Major Tom was in Banja Luka serving with the NATO-led international peacekeeping force, IFOR. From 1992 to 1995 Bosnian Serbs had fought Bosnian Croats and Bosnian Muslims in an attempt to split Bosnia into two hostile territories. In 1995 the U.S.-brokered Dayton Agreement ended the war by splitting Bosnia into two hostile territories. The Federation of Bosnia and Herzegovina was run by Croats and Muslims. The Republika Srpska was run by Serbs. IFOR's job was to "implement and monitor the Dayton Agreement." Major Tom's job was to sit in an office where Croat and Muslim residents of Republika Srpska went to report Dayton Agreement violations.

"They come to me," said Major Tom, "and they say, 'The Serbs stole my car.' And I say, 'I'm writing that in my report.' They say, 'The Serbs burned my house.' And I say, 'I'm writing that in my report.' They say, 'The Serbs raped my daughter.' And I say, 'I'm writing that in my report.'"

"Then what happens?" I said.

"I put my report in a file cabinet."

Major Tom had fought in the Gulf War. He'd been deployed to Haiti during the American reinstatement of President Aristide (which preceded the recent American unreinstatement). He was on his second tour of duty in Bosnia and would go on to fight in the Iraq war. That night we got drunk.

"Please, no nation building," said Major Tom. "We're the Army. We kill people and break things. They didn't teach nation building in infantry school."

Or in journalism school, either. The night before I left to cover the Iraq war I got drunk with another friend, who works in TV news. We were talking about how—as an approach to national security—invading Iraq was . . . different. I'd moved my family from Washington to New Hampshire. My friend was considering getting his family out of New York. "Don't you hope," my friend said, "that all this has been thought through by someone who is smarter than we are?" It is, however, a universal tenet of democracy that no one is.

Americans hate foreign policy. Americans hate foreign policy because Americans hate foreigners. Americans hate foreigners because Americans *are* foreigners. We all come from foreign parts, even if we came ten thousand years ago on a land bridge across the Bering Strait. We didn't want anything to do with those Ice Age Siberians, them with the itchy cave-bear-pelt underwear and mammoth meat on their breath. We were off to the Pacific Northwest—great salmon fishing, blowout potluck dinners, a whole new life.

America is not "globally conscious" or "multicultural." Americans didn't come to America to be Limey Poofters, Frog-Eaters, Bucket Heads, Micks, Spicks, Sheenies, or Wogs. If we'd wanted foreign entanglements, we would have stayed home. Or—in the case of those of us who were shipped to America against our will, as slaves, exiles, or transported prisoners—we would have gone back. Events in Liberia and the type of American who lives in Paris tell us what to think of that.

4

Being foreigners ourselves, we Americans know what foreigners are up to with their foreign policy—their venomous convents, lying alliances, greedy agreements, and trick-or-treaties. America is not a wily, sneaky nation. We don't think that way. We don't think much at all, thank God. Start thinking and pretty soon you get ideas, and then you get idealism, and the next thing you know you've got ideology, with millions dead in concentration camps and gulags. A fundamental American question is "What's the big idea?"

Americans would like to ignore foreign policy. Our previous attempts at isolationism were successful. Unfortunately, they were successful for Hitler's Germany and Tojo's Japan. Evil is an outreach program. A solitary bad person sitting alone, harboring genocidal thoughts, and wishing he ruled the world is not a problem unless he lives next to us in the trailer park. In the big geopolitical trailer park that is the world today, he does.

America has to act. But, when America acts, other nations accuse us of being "hegemonistic," of engaging in "unilateralism," of behaving as if we're the only nation on earth that counts.

We are. Russia used to be a superpower but resigned "to spend more time with the family." China is supposed to be mighty, but the Chinese leadership quakes when a couple of hundred Falun Gong members do tai chi for Jesus. The European Union looks impressive on paper, with a greater population and a larger economy than America's. But the military spending of Britain, France, Germany, and Italy combined does not equal one third of the U.S. defense budget. The United States spends more on defense than the aforementioned countries—plus Russia plus China plus the next six top defense-spending nations. Any multilateral military or diplomatic effort that includes the United States is a crew team with Arnold Schwarzenegger as coxswain and Nadia Comaneci on the oars. When other countries demand a role in the exercise of global power, America can ask another fundamental American question: "You and what army?"

Americans find foreign policy confusing. We are perplexed by the subtle tactics and complex strategies of the Great Game. America's great game is pulling the levers on the slot machines in Las Vegas. We can't figure out what the goal of American foreign policy is supposed to be.

The goal of American tax policy is avoiding taxes. The goal of American health policy is HMO profits. The goal of American environmental policy is to clean up the environment, clearing away scruffy caribou and seals so that America's drillers for Arctic oil don't get trampled or slapped with a flipper. But the goal of American foreign policy is to foster international cooperation, protect Americans at home and abroad, promote world peace, eliminate human rights abuses, improve U.S. business and trade opportunities, and stop global warming.

We were going to stop global warming by signing the Kyoto protocol on greenhouse gas emissions. Then we realized the Kyoto protocol was ridiculous and unenforceable and that no one who signed it was even trying to meet the emissions requirements except for some countries from the former Soviet Union. They accidentally quit emitting greenhouse gases because their economies collapsed. However, if we withdraw from diplomatic agreements because they're ridiculous, we'll have to withdraw from every diplomatic agreement, because they're all ridiculous. This will not foster international cooperation. But if we *do* foster international cooperation, we won't be able to protect Americans at home and abroad, because there has been a lot of international cooperation in killing Americans. Attacking internationals won't promote world peace, which we can't have anyway if we're going to eliminate human rights abuses, because there's no peaceful way to get rid of the governments that abuse the rights of people—people who are chained to American gym-shoe-making machinery, dying of gym shoe lung, and getting paid in shoelaces, thereby improving U.S. business and trade opportunities, which result in economic expansion that causes global warming to get worse.

As the nineteenth-century American naval hero Stephen Decatur said in his famous toast: "Our Country! In her intercourse with foreign nations may she always be in the right; but our country, right or wrong, should carry condoms in her purse."

One problem with changing America's foreign policy is that we keep doing it. After the Cold War, President George H. W. Bush managed to engage America—in spite of itself—in the multilateralism of the Gulf War. This left Saddam Hussein exactly where we found him twelve years later. Like other American achievements in multilateralism, it wasn't something we'd care to achieve again. The east side of midtown Manhattan, where a decent slum once stood, is blighted by the United Nations headquarters. And, in the mountains of the Balkan peninsula, the ghost of Woodrow Wilson wanders Marley-like, dragging his chains and regretting the deeds of his life.

President Bill Clinton dreamed of letting the lion lie down with the lamb chop. Clinton kept International Monetary Fund cash flowing into the ever-criminalizing Russian economy. He ignored Kremlin misbehavior from Boris Yeltsin's shelling of elected representatives in the Duma to Vladimir Putin's airlifting uninvited Russian troops into Kosovo. Clinton compared the Chechnya fighting to the American Civil War (murdered Chechens being on the South Carolina statehouse Confederate-flag-flying side). Clinton called China America's "strategic partner" and paid a nine-day visit to that country, not bothering himself with courtesy calls on America's actual strategic partners, Japan and South Korea. Clinton announced, "We don't support independence for Taiwan," and said of Jiang Zemin, instigator of the assault on democracy protesters in Tiananmen Square, "He has vision."

Anything for peace, that was Clinton's policy. Clinton had special peace-mongering envoys in Cyprus, Congo, the Middle East, the Balkans, and flying off to attend secret talks with Marxist guerrillas in Colombia. Clinton made frantic attempts to close an Israeli-Palestinian peace deal. What if the Jews control the Temple Mount and the Arabs control the movie industry? On his last day in office, Clinton was still phoning Sinn Fein leader Gerry Adams. "Love your work, Gerry. Do you ever actually kill people? Or do you just do the spin?"

Clinton was everybody's best friend. Except when he wasn't. He conducted undeclared air wars against Serbia and Iraq and launched missiles at Sudan and Afghanistan. Clinton used the military more often than any previous peacetime American president. He sent armed forces into areas of conflict on an average of once every nine weeks.

Then we elected an administration with adults in it—Colin Powell, Dick Cheney, and Donald Rumsfeld. Gone was the harum-scarum Clinton policy-making apparatus with its frenzied bakeheads piling up midnight pizza boxes in the Old Executive Office Building. They disappeared, along with the clinically insane confidants—vein-popping James Carville, toe-sucking Dick Morris—and the loose haircuts in the West Wing and the furious harridan on the White House third floor.

President George W. Bush's foreign policy was characterized, in early 2001, as "disciplined and consistent" (—Condoleezza Rice): "blunt" (—*The Washington Post*), and "in-your-face" (—the Carnegie Endowment for International Peace). Bush began his term with the expulsion of one fourth of the Russian diplomatic corps on grounds of espionage. He snubbed Vladimir Putin by delaying a first summit meeting until June 2001, and then holding it in fashionable Slovenia.

On April 1, 2001, a Chinese fighter jet, harassing a U.S. reconnaissance plane in international airspace, collided with the American aircraft, which was forced to land in Chinese territory. Bush did not regard this as an April Fools' prank. By the end of the month he had gone on *Good Morning America* and said that if China attacked Taiwan, the United States had an obligation to defend it.

"With the full force of American military?" asked Charlie Gibson.

"Whatever it took," said Bush.

The president also brandished American missile defenses at Russia and China. The Russians and Chinese were wroth. The missile shield might or might not stop missiles, but, even unbuilt, it was an effective tool for gathering intelligence on Russian and Chinese foreign policy intentions. We knew how things stood when the town drunk and the town bully strongly suggested that we shouldn't get a new home security system.

In the Middle East, Bush made an attempt to let the Israelis and the Palestinians go at it until David ran out of pebbles and Goliath had been hit on the head so many times that he was voting for Likud. In Northern Ireland, Bush also tried minding his own business. And Bush quit negotiating with North Korea about its atomic weapons for the same reason that you'd quit jawing with a crazy person about the gun he was waving and call 911.

We saw the results of Clinton's emotional, ad hoc, higgledy-piggledy foreign policy. It led to strained relations with Russia and China, increased violence in the Middle East, continued fighting in Africa and Asia, and Serbs killing Albanians. Then we saw the results of Bush's tough, calculated, focused foreign policy—strained relations with Russia and China, increased violence in the Middle East, continued fighting in Africa and Asia, and Albanians killing Serbs. Between the first year of the Clinton administration and the first year of the Bush administration, we went from attack on the World Trade Center to World Trade Center attack.

Further changes could be made to U.S. foreign policy. For a sample of alternative ideas, we can turn to a group of randomly (even haphazardly) chosen, average (not to say dull-normal) Americans: the 2004 Democratic presidential hopefuls. By the time this is read, most of them will be forgotten. With luck, all of them will be. Nonetheless, it's instructive to recall what ten people who offered themselves as potential leaders of the world deemed to be America's foreign policy options.

Incessant activist Al Sharpton pleaded for "a policy of befriending and creating allies around the world." The way Sharpton intended to make friends was by fixing the world's toilets and sinks. "There are 1.7 billion people that need clean water," he said, "almost three billion that need sanitation systems . . . I would train engineers . . . would export people that would help with these things."

Ex–child mayor of Cleveland Dennis Kucinich promised to establish "a cabinet-level Department of Peace." The secretary of peace would do for international understanding what the postmaster general does for mail.

Former one-term senator and erstwhile ambassador to New Zealand Carol Moseley Braun said, "I believe women have a contribution to make . . . we are clever enough to defeat terror without destroying our own liberty . . . we can provide for long-term security by making peace everybody's business." Elect me because women are clever busybodies. This is the "Lucy and Ethel Get an Idea" foreign policy.

Massachusetts's thinner, more sober senator, John Kerry, said that he voted for threatening to use force on Saddam Hussein, but that actually using force was wrong. This is what's known, in the language of diplomacy, as bullshit.

Previous almost–vice president Joe Lieberman indignantly demanded that Bush do somewhat more of what Bush already was doing: "Commit more U.S. troops," create "an Iraqi interim authority," and "work with the Iraqi people and the United Nations." Perhaps Lieberman hadn't gotten over coming this close to the office next to the oval one. Perhaps Lieberman was suffering from a delusion that he was part of the current presidential administration. But after 9/11 Americans wanted to kiss the Supreme Court. Imagine having a Democrat as commander in chief during the War Against

Terrorism, with Oprah Winfrey as secretary of defense. Big hug for Mr. Taliban. Republicans are squares, but it's the squares who know how to fly the bombers, launch the missiles, and fire the M-16s. Democrats would still be fumbling with the federally mandated trigger locks. And did Al Gore grow that beard for a while just in case the Taliban won?

Onetime governor of insignificant Vermont Howard Dean wanted a cold war on terrorism. Dean said that we'd won the Cold War without firing a shot (a statement that doubtless surprised veterans of Korea and Vietnam). Dean said that the reason we'd won the Cold War without firing a shot was because we were able to show the communists "a better ideal." But what is the "better ideal" that we can show the Islamic fundamentalists? Maybe we can tell them, "*Our* president is a born-again. You're religious lunatics—*we're* religious lunatics. America was *founded* by religious lunatics! How about those Salem witch trials? Come to America and you could be Osama bin Ashcroft. You could get your own state, like Utah, *run* by religious lunatics. You could have an Islamic Fundamentalist Winter Olympics—the Chador Schuss."

Since the gist of Howard Dean's campaign platform was "It Worked in Vermont," he really may have thought that the terrorists should take up snowboarding. On the other hand, the gist of General (very retired) Wesley Clark's campaign platform was "It Worked in Kosovo." Kosovo certainly taught the world a lesson. Wherever there's suffering, injustice, and oppression, America will show up six months late and bomb the country next to where it's happening.

The winner of South Carolina's JFK look-alike contest, John Edwards, and the winner of Florida's Bob Gramm look-alike contest, Bob Gramm, said that America had won the war in Iraq but was losing the peace because Iraq was so unstable. When Iraq was stable it attacked Israel in 1967 and 1973. It attacked Iran. It attacked Kuwait. It gassed the Kurds. It butchered the Shiites. It fostered terrorism in the Middle East. Who wanted a stable Iraq?

And perennial representative of the House of Representatives Dick Gephardt wouldn't talk much about foreign policy. He was concentrating on economic issues, claiming that he'd make the American Dream come true for everyone. Gephardt may have been on to something there. Once people get rich they don't go in much for war-making. The shoes are ugly and the uniforms itch. Someday Osama bin Laden will call a member of one of his "sleeper cells"—a person who was planted in the United States years before and told to live like a normal American—and . . .

"Dad, some guy named Ozzy's on the phone."

"Oh, uh, good to hear from you. Of course, of course . . . Rockefeller Center? . . . Next Wednesday? . . . I'd love to, but the kid's got her ballet recital. You miss something like that, they never forget it . . . Thursday's no good. I have to see my mom off on her cruise to Bermuda in the morning. It's Fatima's yoga day. And I've got courtside seats for the Nets . . . Friday we're going to the Hamptons for the weekend . . ."

But how, exactly, did Gephardt plan to make everyone on earth as materialistic, self-indulgent, and overscheduled as Americans? Would Gephardt give foreigners options on hot dot-com stocks? That might have worked during the Clinton years.

As of early 2004 there was one foremost, pressing question in U.S. foreign policy, and America didn't seem to have the answers for postwar Iraq. Then again, what were the questions?

Was there a bad man? And his bad kids? Were they running a bad country? That did bad things? Did they have a lot of oil money to do bad things with? Were they going to do more bad things?

If those were the questions, was the answer "UN-supervised national reconciliation" or "Rapid return to self-rule"?

No. The answer was blow the place to bits.

Critics say we didn't do enough thinking about the problem of postwar Iraq. I say we blew the place to bits—what's the problem?

If there is something we didn't do enough thinking about—something we haven't done enough thinking about for sixty years—it's fascism. The genius of fascism is to turn people into a mob. Baath Party fascism did a good job. Fascism doesn't use only the stick; it uses the carrot as well, albeit in a brutal fashion. There's a lot of being hit over the head with root vegetables involved in fascism. But Hitler would have ended up painting carnival sideshow posters in Bavaria if a mob of Germans hadn't thought they were getting something out of fascism. And how do you plan for a mob? Do you buy *The Martha Stewart Book of Gracious Rioting*?

Americans have been surprised by Iraqi fascism, although we are familiar enough with other evil ideologies. Communism still persists in Cuba, North Korea, and the minds of a million university-type intellectuals. Religious extremism waxes worldwide. But communists do bad things for a purpose. They have a vision of a utopia where everyone shares everything and you give your Lawn Boy to a family in Chad. And religious extremists do bad things for a purpose. They have a vision of a utopia where everyone goes to heaven together. So what if you have to die to get there? You have to die to get to heaven anyway. Fascism, however, is a pointless ideology—the grasp of power for power's sake. The fight against fascism seems like Dad's war, Granddad's war. Fascism should be out of date in the purposeful, task-oriented world of today. Never mind Slobodan Milosevic, Vladimir Putin, the Palestinian Authority, Somali warlords, Charles Taylor, China's politburo, the Saudi royal family, murderous Hutu rabble, and Newt Gingrich's career arc.

Fascists do bad things just to be bad. "I'm the baddest dude in Baghdad," Saddam Hussein was saying,"the baddest cat in the Middle East. I'm way bad." This was way stupid. But fascists *are* stupid. Consider Saddam Hussein's weapons of mass destruction. He didn't have any. How stupid does *that* make Saddam? All he had to do was say to UN chief weapons inspector Hans Blix, "Look where you want. Look beneath the couch cushions. Look under my bed. Look in the special spider hole I'm keeping for emergencies." And Saddam Hussein could have gone on dictatoring away until Donald Rumsfeld is elected head of the World Council of Churches.

Instead, we blew the place to bits. And a mess was left behind. But it's a mess without a military to fight aggressive wars; a mess without the facilities to develop dangerous weapons; a mess that cannot systematically kill, torture, and oppress millions of its citizens. It's a mess with a message—don't mess with us.

Saddam Hussein was reduced to the Unabomber, Ted Kaczynski, a nutcase hiding in the sticks. The terrorism his cohorts practice is terrifying, hence its name. Killing innocent people by surprise is not called "A Thousand Points of Light." But as frightening as terrorism is, it's the weapon of losers. When someone detonates a suicide bomb, that person does not have career prospects. And no matter how horrific the terrorist attack, it's conducted by losers. Winners don't need to hijack airplanes. Winners have an air force.

2

KOSOVO

November 1999

America is the winner in the new era of highly moral conflicts—just wars, good wars, wars to end . . . other wars. I covered a couple of these, in Kuwait in 1991 and Somalia in 1993. But I didn't stick around for the aftermaths, and, it will be remembered (especially by Iraqi Shiites of the Basra region), neither did America. It wasn't until the NATO occupation of Kosovo that I got a chance to see what happens when the ancient tradition of invasion is stood on its ear. Contrary to a million years of human instincts, conquest now entails giving rather than taking territory while exploiting the victor's labor and resources to heap booty on the conquered.

* * *

The air war against Yugoslavia had been declared a victory. Kosovo was being run by the UN, NATO, and other forces for good. Forces for good and plenty of them—here are some of the more than three hundred well-meaning organizations that were active in Kosovo at the end of 1999: Humanity First, Emergency Corps of the Order of Malta, Center for Mind Body Medicine, Associazione Amici Dei Bambini, Mother Teresa Society, Saudi Joint Relief Committee, American Jewish Joint Distribution Committee, Iranian Relief Committee, Vietnam Veterans of America Foundation, and the World Society for Protection of Animals. So, could Serbs and Albanians now live together peacefully?

A young Albanian and former Kosovo Liberation Army fighter said yes. Well, what he actually said was, "When you hate this much maybe you would kill them all, but we will try to live with them, which shows what kind of people we are."

Something else that showed what kind of people they are was the "NATO" brand bubble gum for sale locally, with bubblegum cards depicting victims of Serb atrocities, KLA martyrs, Albanian refugees, and a cruise missile direct hit on Serbian police headquarters in Pristina.

But the KLA veteran did not look like someone who had been chewing over blood vengeance since his first Halloween. He looked like a slightly bored, faintly irritated member of a tenant committee. Which he was, except that the committee was petitioning the Norwegian Army instead of a landlord.

"A sewer line is blocked," said the tenant committee chairwoman. "Heating oil supply is low. We need more garbage containers."

"We will not have everything for everyone," said a beleaguered Norwegian infantry captain.

The captain was in Kosovo Polje, site of the Battle of Kosovo, where the Ottoman Turks threw the Serbs out of Kosovo in the first place, in 1389. Now Albanian Kosovars had done it again—this time by squatting rather than fighting, in a housing complex that used to be 80 percent Serb and had become 80 percent Albanian. The Norwegians were on hand to prevent murder, and also to provide more garbage containers.

"The level of hatred will always exist," said the KLA veteran. "But we are a peaceful nation and we will try to live with them—if the people who did bad things are punished."

"Thank you for controlling the youths who were throwing stones," said the Norwegian captain.

"We try," said the chairwoman.

Battle-hardened combatants beating their swords into complaints about water pressure and their spears into requests to fix the electrical wiring—it was a dream conflict for liberals, a peace-on-earth, goodwill-to-men, Kris Kringle of a military action. Kosovo was the war the war-haters loved. Bianca Jagger, Susan Sontag, Barney Frank, House Democratic Whip David Bonior, the late Minnesota senator Paul Wellstone, and various other usually reliable advocates of peace seemed to have been drinking at the VFW Hall and getting "Semper Fi" tattooed on their biceps. "I harbor no second thoughts on the morality of our course," Senator Wellstone said. "My only regret is that our action has been less effective than I would have hoped."

Such a regret, of course, depends upon what was hoped *for*. If we hoped to increase wartime destruction, we were very effective. Normally the victor in a war does most of the damage, but in Kosovo everybody got to destroy things—losers, winners, and neutral nations alike.

The locals explained how to tell the difference between the piles of rubble. When the destruction was general, it was Serbian. Serbs surrounded Albanian villages and shelled them. When the destruction was specific, it was Albanian. Albanians set fire to Serb homes and businesses. And when the destruction was pointless—involving a bridge to nowhere, an empty oil storage tank, an evacuated Serb police headquarters, and the like—it was NATO trying to fight a war without hurting anybody.

However, if we hoped to protect ethnic Albanians, we were, as Senator Wellstone mentioned, less effective. In fact, we were less effective at protecting ethnic Albanians than Slobodan Milosevic had been. According to the U.S. State Department, an estimated ten thousand Albanians were killed and 1.5 million were expelled from their homes, most of them *after* the NATO air war began.

On the road from Pec to Istok, in the hills of northwest Kosovo, every single building had been destroyed. Beside the highway, in a gravel patch leveled by a bulldozer, were the graves of nineteen members of the Imeraj family: men, women, and children. The tombs were covered by a type of floral arrangement particular to Kosovo. This is a thin, yardwide disk of foliage with brightly colored blossoms sprinkled on the green background and the whole wrapped tightly in cellophane. Muslim Albanians naturally have no Yuletide decorating tradition and wouldn't understand the horrible free association caused in an American mind—And to all a good night!—by these mementos of the Santa War, these giant Christmas cookies of death.

We failed to protect Albanians from Serbs, but we were making up for it by protecting Serbs from Albanians, even though it was Serb persecution of Albanians that caused us to come to Kosovo, thereby giving Albanians an opportunity to persecute Serbs.

In a background briefing a British colonel said, "Out of a prewar Serbian population of thirty thousand, there are eight hundred and seventy-five Serbs left in Pristina."

"Exactly eight hundred and seventy-five?" I asked.

"Exactly." And (more visions of Saint Nick as NATO Supreme Allied Commander, Europe) the colonel knew when the Serbs were sleeping. He knew when they were awake. He had 250 of his men living with the Serbs.

"Living with them and doing what?" I asked.

"Keeping them alive."

Sometimes. On November 29, 1999, three elderly Serbs were pulled from their car in central Pristina. The man was killed, the two women were severely beaten. On October 11, 1999, an Albanian passerby asked a Bulgarian UN worker, in Serbian, "What time is it?" The Bulgarian replied in Bulgarian, a language too similar to Serbian. He was shot to death.

But the forces for good were agreed that Serbs should stay in Kosovo. And so were the forces for bad. Milosevic wanted Serbs in Kosovo so he could claim that Kosovo was still part of Serbia. NATO wanted Serbs in Kosovo because, when you're fighting a war to save lives, you've got to save somebody's. The UN definitely wanted Serbs in Kosovo. If you don't like multiculturalism, why have a UN? And Senator Paul

Wellstone wanted Serbs in Kosovo to show how wonderful multiculturalism can be—if you've got forty-two thousand troops to enforce it.

Six of those troops were bivouacked in an apartment in downtown Pristina to safeguard twenty-four-year-old Maria, two floors up, the last remaining Serb in the building. This was not bad duty. Maria was beautiful. And her mother, visiting from exile in Serbia, was cute, too. It would be a hard test in bigotry for a normal man to hate this pair. Some of the local fellows managed to pass. "What time is it?" they asked Maria on the street.

I asked Maria, "How do you see your future in Kosovo?"

"I don't see it at all," she said. "I just sold my flat. I'm moving to Belgrade."

"Is there any future for Serbs in Kosovo?"

"No."

In perfect agreement with Maria was the KLA commander of the Lap region of northeast Kosovo, Major General Mustafa Remi. That is, Remi would have been a major general except that the KLA was demilitarized and had been disarmed.

"There hasn't been a disarmament," said General (or whatever) Remi, who was wearing a pistol and being saluted by Albanians. "We have only stored our weapons."

I brought up the subject of UN Resolution 1244. This is the piece of paper that set NATO upon the Serbs. The resolution states, with an interesting choice of verb, that "Kosovo can enjoy substantial autonomy within the Federal Republic of Yugoslavia."

"Does the KLA," I asked the general, "still aspire to an independent Kosovo?"

"We don't *aspire*," said Remi, doing his best—which was very good—to look scary. "We see an independent Kosovo as a reality."

"What if the Western nations don't support this?"

Remi's logic was sound: "I think we are having their support, considering the support that they are offering us."

At Camp Bondsteel, the U.S. headquarters in Kosovo, I interviewed a more affable officer. Camp Bondsteel was an eight-hundred-acre fortified compound in southern Kosovo housing thirty-five hundred U.S. soldiers atop a ridge that dominated a hundred square miles of rolling farmland. At night Bondsteel was lit the way the city on the hill of the Gospels would have been lit if they'd had diesel generators in Saint Matthew's time. By day the earthen tracks and paths were being turned into gravel roads. The tents were being replaced with wooden barracks. The only sewage treatment plant in Kosovo had been built.

"I think the conflict is not over yet," General Remi had told me.

The American officer said, "We learned a lesson in Bosnia. Tents only last three winters."

I asked the officer, "Can you *really* turn this place into a multicultural society?"

"We'll try our best. After all," said the officer with an optimistic, very American smile, "if anybody can do it, *we* can."

Which, back in America we, rather famously, can't.

A bored black private stood guard at another American fortress, Camp Monteith, in southeastern Kosovo. On the subject of local hatreds, he said, "At least if they put you and me in a police lineup, they can tell us apart."

* * *

But they can tell Maria, too. "Serbs are identifiable," said Maria. "I can't explain why. It's subtle—facial structure." She told me about a ten-year-old boy, walking down the street, who pulled a knife on her and said, "You are Serb. I kill you." Maria's mother said a little kid ran up to her and pantomimed a throat-slitting.

Maybe it's the bubble gum. Or maybe it's history. Peoples who hate each other often seem to be fond of history. The Serbs, the Serbs say, have always been in Kosovo. Except that the Serbs didn't arrive in the Balkans until the sixth century A.D. So Albanians, the Albanians say, have always been in Kosovo. Although British historian Miranda Vickers says, "Serbian archaeologists have been hard at work seeking to refute . . . the long-standing Albanian claim for a continuity of descent from the ancient Ilyrians." Anyway, somebody's always been in Kosovo. And somebody else is always showing up, the way the Ottoman Turks did in 1389. The Battle of Kosovo caused a large portion of Kosovo's Serbs to leave for, among other places, Transylvania (making one wonder why the Serbs don't hate vampires rather than ethnic Albanians).

The Serbs reconquered Kosovo in 1912 and committed atrocities against the Albanians, who sided with Germany in 1914 and oppressed the Serbs, who regained control of Kosovo in 1918 and tyrannized the Albanians, who sided with the Germans again in 1939 and crushed the Serbs, who recaptured Kosovo in 1945 and persecuted the Albanians, who rioted in 1981 and beat and robbed the Serbs, who . . .

"Oh," said Maria's mother to Maria with an I-forgot-to-feed-the-cat look, "you got another threatening phone call. A man's voice said, 'What are you waiting for?'"

Food aid was the answer to that question in Gorazdevac, a Serb village in western Kosovo that once had a population of 2,000. The number of residents shrank to about 30 during the air war but had now returned to . . . "Eight hundred," said the village drunk, although 770 seem to be making themselves scarce.

The village headman—or, anyway, the oldest male around—explained that it took five soldiers from the Italian armored brigade in Pec to escort a single villager into the fields. As a result, no winter wheat had been planted, there wasn't enough livestock fodder to last until spring, and—he grew grave—"Yesterday a haystack was set on fire."

"How are people living?" I asked.

"Food aid," he said, serving the Italian soldiers, a son-in-law, me, and the village drunk morning glasses of Sljivovica Manastirka that, if you missed your mouth, could provide a skin peel and an eyelid tuck.

"Can Serbs and Albanians live together peacefully?" I asked.

"We would like to live as before the war," said the headman. "Even though in the past we didn't want to live together, we lived together."

"There is only one God above us!" said the village drunk.

I asked if the Milosevic government had been unfair to the Albanians.

The headman's son-in-law answered. "Milosevic called for Albanians and Serbs to live together." Two little boys peeked shyly at the yakking men. The son-in-law said he'd named them "Wolf" and "Fearless."

"The Albanians would start a war anyway," said the son-in-law.

The village was a Peter Brueghel painting, if you ignored the villagers in Nikes and the corrugated metal and concrete block that augmented the thatch and the wattle-and-daub. A listing half-timbered gristmill sat athwart a stream. The stream wandered through the main road, and so did pigs.

"The cultural level of Albanians is low. Serbian culture is more high," said the son-in-law.

Luan Mulliqi, the new Albanian director of Kosovo's national Galeria e Arteve—which was up and running in Pristina, although things like water and electricity often weren't—said, "What is a difficult place to live is, for culture, heaven."

Mulliqi was giving me a tour, partly by flashlight, of an exhibit of Kosovar Albanian modern art. Intimations of dread and portraits of corpses pervaded the pictures, although most were painted a quarter of a century before, when Yugoslavia was supposedly a multicultural model to the world. Even the abstracts look worried. One of these was gloomy and terrifying without anything on the canvas except a white billowing shape. "A shroud," said Mulliqi.

The recent artworks, created during the previous year's chaos, were more cheerful. Mulliqi, himself a sculptor, was finishing a piece that incorporated a swatch of the green Astroturf of hope, an array of the tools of reconstruction, and some new wood rafters fastened to an old charred roof beam. A corpse was hanging from those rafters, but it was a cheerful sculpture, comparatively speaking.

Serbs argued that Kosovo's Albanians were cheerful because they were enjoying their martyrdom. "An Albanian with seven sons will sacrifice six for Albanian independence," said the village drunk in Gorazdevac (perhaps making poor young Wolf and Fearless think, "Don't give Dad ideas.")

More likely what Kosovo's Albanians were enjoying was a chance to provide martyrdom to Serbs, especially their immediate neighbors. "Crimes in Kosovo were done by Serbs *here*," said the KLA vet in Kosovo Polje. "No Serb in Belgrade would know which house Albanians lived in."

In Pasjane, another of Kosovo's Serb villages, the school principal begged to differ, at least about the behavior of the Serbs in his hometown. "There was no killing," he said. "There was no looting." He paused. A large photograph of Slobodan Milosevic hung on his office wall. "Well, maybe there was some. But all the dirty people ran away to Serbia. The people remaining in Pasjane are all honest, decent people."

Honest, decent, and furious. Pasjane, in the far southeast of Kosovo, was under intermittent mortar attack from Albanians in the surrounding hills who hadn't gotten the news about storing their weapons. A man had been killed two days before. The other men in Pasjane left the funeral and gathered in the churchyard. They pointed to gravestones damaged by mortar attacks. They pointed to the shrapnel scars on the church.

"This church is from the 1200s."

"This village is from 1340."

"First to fight the Turks."

"Before 1389 all these villages were Serb."

Old hatreds aside, new hatreds were growing apace—hatred for the Americans guarding Pasjane, for example. A U.S. Army forensics team had come to gather the shell fragments from the lethal mortar attack. The Pasjane Serbs said that they believed the U.S. Army did this to hide something. When the man was killed, they said, an American armored personnel carrier was down the road. The APC turned off its engine just before the mortar shell struck. The Pasjane Serbs thought the U.S. Army was giving a signal to hidden Albanians.

Why couldn't everyone cooperate in Kosovo the way Russian troops and NATO troops were cooperating, which, according to official military sources with whom I spoke, was "fully," even if the Russians had arrived as peacekeeping gate-crashers and even if the Russians were supposed to be perpetrating in Chechnya what the Russians were supposed to be preventing in Kosovo and even if, as one Norwegian enlisted man said unofficially, "the Russians drink on duty"?

"Time is the best medicine," said a colonel in the Russian medical corps who was running a civilian clinic in Kosovo Polje.

"If time is the best medicine," I said, "why don't we all feel better than we did twenty years ago?"

"That," the colonel said, "is a good question."

Another good question was: What really should be done with the Serbs and Albanians? One British soldier, on night patrol through a former Serbian—now sooty ruin—

section of Pristina, said, "It's what barbed wire was invented for."

But advocating barbed wire would have embarrassed the forces for good, the participants in the peace blitzkrieg, the elves in the Santa War. So the tenant committee meetings went on.

"We'd like you to take down the Albanian flag on the balcony," said the beleaguered Norwegian captain in Kosovo Polje. "It could be seen as a provocation."

"It's a wedding tradition," said the chairwoman.

"The wedding was last week."

"Flying the flag from Thursday to Monday—that is the tradition," said the KLA veteran.

"Well, tomorrow is Tuesday," said the captain. "And one more thing. There are too many stray dogs. They are creating a health problem . . ."

Said an Italian colonel in Pec, "This is the future of war."

3

ISRAEL

April 2001

Passover is my idea of a perfect holiday. Dear God, when you're handing out plagues of darkness, locusts, hail, boils, flies, lice, frogs, and cattle murrain, and turning the Nile to blood, and smiting firstborn, give me a pass, and tell me when it's over.

And the Lord did well by me at Passover—brilliant sunshine on the beaches of Tel Aviv, pellucid waters, no flies in my room at the Hilton, and certainly no lice. I am a firstborn myself but was not the least smitten, not even by the cute waitress at the Hilton's kosher sushi restaurant. I am a happily married man. And by the way, Leviticus 11:10 says, "Of any living thing which is in the waters, they shall be an abomination unto you," an apt description of sushi as far as I'm concerned. But gentiles aren't expected to understand the intricacies of dietary law, although extra complications thereof lead to Passover's main drawback: food and—more important to gentiles—drink.

"I'll have a scotch," I said to the Hilton's bartender.

"Scotch isn't kosher for Passover," he said. "It's made with leaven."

"Gin and tonic," I said.

"Gin isn't kosher."

"What can I have?"

"You can have a screwdriver—Israeli vodka and orange juice."

"What's Israeli vodka like?" I asked.

"The orange juice is very good."

There was no plague of tourists in Israel. It should have been a period of hectic visitation, with Passover beginning April 7 and the Eastern Orthodox and Western Easters coinciding a week later. But Israel's income from tourism dropped 58 percent in the last quarter of 2000, and to judge by the lineless queues at Ben-Gurion Airport and the empty-seated aisles of El Al, the drop had continued. The marble lobby of the Hilton echoed, when at all, with the chatter of idle desk clerks and bellhops. The din of strife had rendered Israel quiet.

Quiet without portentous hush—traffic hum, A.C. buzz, and cell phone beepings indicated ordinary life in an ordinary place. Tourism wasn't the only thing there was no sign of in Israel. Demonstrations didn't block intersections, public address systems failed to crackle with imperatives, exigent posters weren't stuck to walls, except to advertise raves. There was no sign of crisis—international or bilateral or domestic political—although all news reports agreed that a crisis raged here, and an economic crisis as well. A 12 percent quarterly decline in gross domestic product was unevident in boarded-up shops and empty cafés, which didn't exist, or in beggars and homeless, who weren't on the streets.

There was no sign of terrorism, not that there hadn't been some. But what doesn't inspire terror, by definition, isn't terrorism. The Carmel Market was crowded, either with people wholly unafraid or with people indifferent to whether they were blown up singly or in bunches. If security was pervasive, it was invisible. Israel, I've heard, is hated fanatically by millions of Muslims around the world, whereas the U.S. Congress is loathed by only a small number of well-informed people who follow politics closely. But a walk around anything in Israel is less impeded by barriers and armed guards than a walk around the Capitol Building in Washington.

There was no sign of war. Plenty of soldiers were to be seen, carrying their weapons, but this is no shock to the frequent traveler. For all that the world looks askance at America's lack of gun control, foreigners love to wave guns around. Nothing about the Israeli Defense Forces is as odd as Italian carabinieri brandishing their machine pistols while grimly patrolling that flashpoint, Venice.

There was, in fact, no sign of anything in Tel Aviv. In particular there was no sign of Israel's vital importance to world peace—except, of course, those signs of vital importance to world peace that one sees everywhere, the lettering here in Hebrew but the trademark logos recognizable enough.

Tel Aviv is new, built on the sand dunes north of Jaffa in the 1890s, about the same time Miami was founded. The cities bear a resemblance in size, site, climate, and architecture ranging from the bland to the fancifully bland. In Miami the striving, somewhat troublesome immigrant population is the result of Russia's meddling with Cuba. In Tel Aviv the striving, somewhat troublesome immigrant population is the result of Russia's meddling with itself. I found a Russian restaurant where they couldn't have cared less what was made with leaven, where they had scotch, and where, over one scotch too many, I contemplated the absurdity of Israel being an ordinary place.

What if people who had been away for ages, out and on their own, suddenly showed up at their old home and demanded to move back in? My friends with grown-up children tell me this happens all the time. What if the countless ancient tribal groups that are now defeated, dispersed, and stateless contrived to reestablish themselves in their ancestral lands in such a way as to dominate everyone around them? The Mashantucket Pequots are doing so this minute at their Foxwoods casino in southeastern Connecticut. What if a religious group sought a homeland, never minding how multifarious its religion had become or how divergent its adherents were in principles and practices? A homeland for Protestants would have to satisfy the aspirations of born-again literalists holding forth about creationism in their concrete-block tabernacles and also fulfill the hopes and dreams of vaguely churched latitudinarians giving praise to God's creation by playing golf on Sundays. A Protestant Zion would need to be perfect both for sniping at abortion doctors in North Carolina and for marrying lesbians in Vermont. As an American, I already live in that country.

Maybe there's nothing absurd about Israel. I wandered out into the ordinary nighttime, down Jabotinsky Street, named after the founder of Revisionist Zionism, Ze'ev Jabotinsky, who wrote in 1923, "A voluntary agreement between us and the Arabs of Palestine is inconceivable now or in the foreseeable future." Thus Jabotinsky broke with the father of Zionism, Theodor Herzl, who, in *Altneuland* (1902), had a fictional future Arab character in a fictional future Israel saying, "The Jews have made us prosperous, why should we be angry with them?" And now the Carmel Market was full of goods from Egypt.

From Jabotinsky Street I meandered into Weizmann Street, named for the first president of Israel, Chaim Weizmann, who in 1919 met with Emir Faisal, future king of Iraq and a son of the sharif of Mecca, and concluded an agreement that "all necessary measures shall be taken to encourage and stimulate immigration of Jews into Palestine on a large scale." Faisal sent a letter to the American Zionist delegates at the Versailles peace conference wishing Jews "a most hearty welcome home."

Turning off Weizmann Street, I got lost for a while among signpost monikers I didn't recognize but that probably commemorated people who became at least as embattled as Jabotinsky, Herzl, Weizmann, and Faisal. I emerged on Ben-Gurion Avenue. The first prime minister of Israel was a ferocious battler. He fought the British mandate, the war of liberation, Palestinian guerrillas, and the Sinai campaign. He even won, most of the time, in the Israeli Knesset. And still he was on the lookout for peace. In the months leading up to the Suez crisis, in 1956, President Dwight Eisenhower had a secret emissary shuttling between Jerusalem and Cairo. Egypt's president, Gamal Abdel Nasser, told the emissary (in words that Yasir Arafat could use and, for all I know, has), "If the initiative [Nasser] was now taking in these talks was known in public he would be faced not only with a political problem, but—possibly—with a bullet."

A bullet was what Yitzhak Rabin got, at the end of Ben-Gurion Avenue, from a Jewish extremist, during a peace rally in the square that now bears Rabin's name. A bullet was also what Emir Faisal's brother, King Abdullah of Jordan, got, from a Muslim extremist, for advocating peace with Israel. Nasser's successor, Anwar Sadat, got a bullet, too.

If bullets were the going price for moderation here-abouts, then I needed another drink. I walked west along Gordon Street—named, I hope, for Judah Leib Gordon, the nineteenth-century Russian novelist who wrote in classical Hebrew, and not for Lord George Gordon, the fanatical anti-Catholic and leader of the 1780 Gordon riots, who converted to Judaism late in life and died in Newgate Prison praising the French Revolution. This brought me to the stretch of nightclubs along the beach promenade. Here, two months later, a suicide bomber would kill twenty-two people outside the Dolphi disco. Most of the victims were teenage Russian girls, no doubt very moderate about everything other than clothes, makeup, and boyfriends.

My tour guide arrived the next morning. His name was a long collection of aspirates, glottal stops, and gutturals with, like printed Hebrew, no evident vowels. "Americans can never pronounce it," he said. "Just call me T'zchv."

I called him Z. I was Z's only customer. He drove a minibus of the kind that in the United States always seems to be filled with a church group. And so was Z's, until recently. "Most of my clients," he said, "are the fundamentalists. They want to go everywhere in the Bible. But now . . ." The people who talk incessantly about the Last Days have quit visiting the place where the world will end, due to violence in the region.

Z was seventy-five, a retired colonel in the Israeli Defense Forces, a veteran of every war from liberation to the invasion of Lebanon. "Our worst enemy is CNN," he said. His parents had come from Russia in 1908 and settled on the first kibbutz in Palestine. Z was full of anger about the fighting in Israel—the fighting with the ultra-Orthodox Jews. "They don't serve in the army. They don't pay taxes. The government gives them money. I call them Pharisees."

As we walked around, Z would greet people of perfectly secular appearance by name, adding, "You Pharisee, you," or would introduce me to someone in a T-shirt and jeans who had, maybe, voted for Ariel Sharon in the most recent election by saying, "I want you to meet Moshe, a real Pharisee, this one."

Z said over and over, "The problem is with the Pharisees." About Arabs I couldn't get him to say much. Z seemed to regard Arabs as he did weather. Weather is important. Weather is good. We enjoy weather. We respect weather. Nobody likes to be out in weather when it gets dramatic. "My wife won't let me go to the Palestinian areas," Z said.

"Let's go to an ultra-Orthodox neighborhood," I said.

"You don't want to go there," he said. "They're dumps. You want to see where Jesus walked by the Sea of Galilee."

"No, I don't."

"'And Jesus, walking by the sea of Galilee, saw two brethren, Simon called Peter, and Andrew his brother, casting a net into the sea' . . ." For a man at loggerheads with religious orthodoxy, Z recited a lot of scripture, albeit mostly New Testament, where Pharisees come off looking pretty bad. When quoting, Z would shift to the trochaic foot—familiar to him, perhaps, from the preaching of his evangelical tourists; familiar to me from Mom yelling through the screen door, "*You get in here right this minute!*"

As a compromise we went to Jaffa and had Saint Peter's fish from the Sea of Galilee for lunch. Jaffa is the old port city for Jerusalem, a quaint jumble of Arab architecture out of which the Arabs ran or were run (depending on who's writing history) during Israel's war of liberation. Like most quaint jumbles adjacent to quaintness-free cities, Jaffa is full of galleries and studios. Israel is an admirably artsy place. And, as in other artsy places of the contemporary world, admiration had to be aimed principally at the effort. The output indicated that Israelis should have listened when God said, "Thou shalt not make unto thee any graven image, or any likeness of any thing." Some of the abstract stuff was good.

I wanted to look at art. Z wanted me to look at the house of Simon the Tanner, on the Jaffa waterfront. This, according to Acts 10:10–15, is where Saint Peter went into a trance and foresaw a universal Christian church and, also, fitted sheets. Peter had a vision of "a great sheet knit at the four corners, and let down to the earth: Wherein were all manner of fourfooted beasts of the earth, and wild beasts, and creeping things." God told Peter to kill them and eat them. Peter thought this didn't look kosher—or probably, in the case of the creeping things, appetizing. And God said that what He had cleansed should not be called unclean.

"Then is when Peter knew Christianity was for everyone, not just the Jews!" said Z with vicarious pride in another religion's generous thought.

A little too generous. To Peter's idea we owe ideology, the notion that the wonderful visions we have involve not only ourselves but the whole world, whether the world wants to be involved or not. Until that moment of Peter's in Jaffa, the killing of heretics and infidels was a local business. Take, for example, the case of John the Baptist: with Herodias, Herod Antipas, and stepdaughter Salome running the store, it was a mom-and-pop operation. But by the middle of the first century theological persecution had gone global in the known world. Eventually the slaughter would outgrow the limited market in religious differences. In the twentieth century millions of people were murdered on purely intellectual grounds.

"Can we go in?" I asked.

"No," Z said, " the Muslims put a mosque in there, which made the Orthodox angry. They rioted, which kept the Christians out. So the police closed the place."

For those who dislike ideology, what's interesting about kibbutzim is that they're such a bad idea. Take an Eastern European intelligentsia and make the desert bloom. One would sooner take Mormons and start a rap label. But Kibbutz Yad Mordechai, three quarters of a mile north of the Gaza Strip, passed the test of ideology. It worked—something no fully elaborated, universally applicable ideology ever does.

I'd never been to a kibbutz. I don't know what I expected—Grossinger's with guns? A bar mitzvah with tractors? Some of my friends went to kibbutzim in the 1960s and came back with tales of sex and socialism. But you could get that at Oberlin, without the circle dancing. I'm sure my polisci-major pals were very little help with the avocado crop. Anyway, what I wasn't expecting was a cluster of JFK-era summer cottages with haphazard flower beds, sagging badminton nets, and Big Wheel tricycles on the grass—Lake Missaukee, Michigan, without Lake Missaukee.

A miniature Michigan of shrubbery and trees covered the low hills of the settlement, but with a network of drip-irrigation lines weaving among the stems and trunks. Here were the fiber-optic connections of a previous and more substantive generation of high-tech visionaries, who meant to treat a troubled world with water (per Al Sharpton) rather than information. Scattered in the greenery were the blank metal-sided workshops and warehouses of present-day agriculture, suggestive more of light industry than of peasanthood. Yad Mordechai has light industry, too, producing housewares and decorative ceramics. Plus it has the largest apiary in Israel, an educational center devoted to honey and bees, a gift shop, a kosher restaurant, and, of all things, thirteen hundred yards from the Gaza Strip, a petting zoo.

Yad Mordechai was founded in 1943 on an untilled, sand-drifted patch of the Negev. The land was bought from the sheik of a neighboring village. And there, in the humble little verb of the preceding sentence, is the moral genius of Zionism. Theodor Herzl, when he set down the design of

Zionism in *The Jewish State* (1896), wrote, "The land . . . must, of course, be privately acquired." The Zionists intended to buy a nation rather than conquer one. This had never been tried. Albeit various colonists, such as the American ones, had foisted purchase-and-sale agreements on peoples who had no concept of fee-simple tenure or of geography as anything but a free good. But the Zionists wanted an honest title search.

More than a hundred years ago the Zionists realized what nobody has realized yet—nobody but a few cranky Austrian economists and some very rich people skimming the earth in Gulfstream jets. Nothing is zero-sum, not even statehood. Man can make more of everything, including the very thing he sets his feet on, as the fellow getting to his feet and heading to the bar on the G-V can tell you. "If we wish to found a State to-day," Herzl wrote, "we shall not do it in the way which would have been the only possible one a thousand years ago."

Whether the early Zionists realized what they'd realized is another matter. Palestinian Arabs realized, very quickly, that along with the purchased polity came politics. In politics, as opposed to reality, everything is zero-sum.

Considering how things are going politically in Zion these days, the foregoing quotation from Herzl should be continued and completed.

> Supposing, for example, we were obliged to clear a country of wild beasts, we should not set about the task in the fashion of Europeans of the fifth century. We should not take spear and lance and go out singly in pursuit of bears; we should organize a large and lively hunting party, drive the animals together, and throw a melinite bomb into their midst.

On May 19, 1948, Yad Mordechai was attacked by an Egyptian armored column with air and artillery support. The kibbutz was guarded by 130 men and women, some of them teenagers, most without military training. They had fifty-five light weapons, one machine gun, and a two-inch mortar. Yad Mordechai held out for six days—long enough for the Israeli Army to secure the coast road to Tel Aviv. Twenty-six of the defenders were killed, along with about three hundred Egyptians.

A slit trench has been left along the Yad Mordechai hilltop, with the original fifty-five weapons fastened to boards and preserved with tar. Under the viscous coatings a nineteenth-century British rifle was discernible, and the sink-trap plumbing of two primitive Bren guns. The rest of the firearms looked like the birds and cats that were once mummified—by Egyptians, appropriately enough. Below the trench is a negligee lace of barbed wire, all the barbed wire the kibbutz had in 1948, and beyond that are Egyptian tanks, just where they stopped when they could go no farther. Between the tanks dozens of charging Egyptian soldiers are represented by life-size black-painted two-dimensional cutouts—Gumby commandos, lawn ornaments on attack.

It was the only war memorial I've seen that was both frightening and silly—things all war memorials should be. Most war memorials are sad or awful—things, come to think of it, that war memorials should be also. And this war memorial had a price of admission—which, considering the cost of war, is another good idea.

At the ticket booth was a crabby old guy whom Z greeted with warm complaining, grouch to grouch. Then Z took me to Yad Mordechai's Holocaust museum, which skips pity and goes immediately to Jewish resistance during World War II and Jewish fighting in Palestine and Israel. Yad Mordechai is named for Mordechai Anielewicz, commander of the Warsaw ghetto uprising. The message of the Yad Mordechai museum is that the Holocaust memorial is in the trench at the other end of the kibbutz.

This is the second wonderful thing about Zionism: it was right. Every other "ism" of the modern world was wrong about the nature of civilized man—Marxism, mesmerism, surrealism, pacifism, existentialism, nudism. But civilized man did want to kill Jews, and was going to do more of it. And Zionism was specific. While other systems of thought blundered around in the universal, looking for general solutions to comprehensive problems, Zionism stuck to its guns, or—in the beginning, anyway—to its hoes, mattocks, and irrigation pipes.

True, Zionism has a utopian socialist aspect that is thoroughly nutty as far as I'm concerned. But it's not my concern. No one knocks on my door during dinner and asks me to join a kibbutz or calls me on the weekend to persuade me to drop my current long-distance carrier and make all my phone calls by way of Israel. And given my last name, they won't.

My last name is, coincidently, similar to the maiden name of the Holocaust museum docent, who was Baltimore Irish and had married a young man from the kibbutz and moved there in the 1970s. "I converted," she said, "which the Orthodox make it hard to do, but I went through with it. There's a crabby old guy here who sort of took me under his wing. The first Yom Kippur after I converted, he asked me, 'Did you fast?' I said yes. He said, 'Stupid!' You probably saw him on the way in, behind the ticket counter. He's a veteran of the fight for Yad Mordechai. There's a photo of him here,

when they liberated the kibbutz, in November 'forty-eight."
And there was the photo of the young, heroic, crabby old
guy. And now he was behind the ticket counter at the war
memorial—not making a political career in Jerusalem or writing a book about the young, heroic days, or flogging his story
to the History Channel.

"How cool is that?" said the Baltimore Irish woman running the Holocaust museum.

Z and I had lunch at the kibbutz's self-serve restaurant, where
Z took his plate of meat and sat in the middle of the dairy
section. In the sky to the south we could see smoke rising
from the Gaza Strip—tires burning at an intifada barricade,
or just trash being incinerated. Public services weren't what
they might be in the Palestinian Authority at the moment.
Or maybe it was one of the Jewish settlements in Gaza being
attacked, although we hadn't heard gunfire.

These settlements aren't farms but, mostly, apartment
clusters. "Are the settlements in the West Bank and Gaza some
kind of postagricultural, postindustrial, high-rise Zionism?"
I asked Z. "Or are they a government-funded, mondo-condo,
live-dangerously parody of nation-building?"

"Pharisees!" said Z and went back to eating.

After lunch we drove to Ben-Gurion's house in Tel Aviv,
a modest, foursquare, utterly unadorned structure. But the
inside was cozy with twenty thousand books, in Hebrew,
English, French, German, Russian, Latin, Spanish, Turkish,
and ancient Greek. No fiction, however: a man who devoted
his life to making a profound change in society was uninter-
ested in the encyclopedia of society that fiction provides.

Looking at the thick walls and heavy shutters, I wondered if the house had been built to be defended. Then I twigged to the purpose of the design and gained true respect for the courage of the Zionist pioneers. Ben-Gurion came to the Middle East before air-conditioning was invented—and from Plonsk, at that.

We spent the next day, at my insistence and to Z's mystification, driving around the most ordinary parts of Israel, which look so ordinary to an American that I'm rendered useless for describing them to other Americans. American highway strip-mall development hasn't quite reached Israel, however, so there's even less of the nondescript to not describe.

Z and I stood in a garden-apartment complex in Ashdod, in the garden part, a patch of trampled grass. "Here is the ugliest living in Israel," said Z. We went to a hill on the Ashdod shore, a tell actually, a mound of ancient ruins, an ash heap of history from which we had a view of . . . ash heaps, and the power plant that goes with them, which supplies half of Israel's electricity. Ashdod, incidentally, is a Philistine place-name, not a pun. We could also see the container port, Israel's principal deep-water harbor. "This is the place where the whale threw Jonah up," Z said.

We went to the best suburbs of Tel Aviv, which look like the second-best suburbs of San Diego. We spent a lot of time stuck in traffic. Violence in the West Bank had forced traffic into bottlenecks on Routes 2 and 4 along the coast, in a pattern familiar to anyone negotiating Washington, D.C.'s Beltway—living in a place where you're scared to go to half of it and the other half you can't get to.

Israel is slightly smaller than New Jersey. Moses in effect led the tribes of Israel out of the District of Columbia, parted Chesapeake Bay near Annapolis, and wandered for forty years in Delaware. From the top of Mount Nebo, in the equivalent of Pennsylvania, the Lord showed Moses all of Canaan. New Canaan is in Connecticut—but close enough. And there is a Mount Nebo in Pennsylvania, although it overlooks the Susquehanna rather than the promised land of, say, Paramus. Joshua blew the trumpet, and the malls of Paramus came tumbling down. Israel also has beaches that are at least as attractive as New Jersey's.

An old friend of mine, Dave Garcia, flew in from Hong Kong to spend Easter in Jerusalem. "I like to go places when the tourists aren't there," he said. Dave spent two years in Vietnam when the tourists weren't there, as a prisoner of the Viet Cong. "Let's see where the Prince of Peace was born," he said. "It's in the middle of the intifada."

Z drove us from Ben-Gurion Airport to the roadblock between Jerusalem and Bethlehem. The highway was strewn with broken bottles, as if in the aftermath not of war but of a bad party. Israeli soldiers and Palestinian Authority policemen stood around warily. Z handed us over to an Arab tour-guide friend of his who drove a twenty-five-year-old Mercedes and looked glum. Israel had lost half its tourism, but hotels in Palestinian areas were reporting occupancy rates of 4 percent.

The Arab guide parked at random in the middle of empty Manger Square, outside the Church of the Nativity. "There is normally a three-and-a-half-hour wait," he said as we walked straight into the Manger Grotto. The little cave has been rendered a soot hole by millennia of offertory candles. It's hung with damp-stained tapestries and tarnished lamps and festoons of grimy ornamentation elaborate enough for a Byzantine emperor if the Byzantine emperor lived in the basement. I imagine the Virgin Mary had the place done up more cheerfully, with little homey touches, when it was a barn.

The only other visitors were in a tour group from El Salvador, wearing bright yellow T-shirts and acting cheerfully pious. Dave asked them in Spanish if, after all that El Salvador had been through with earthquakes and civil war, the fuss about violence and danger around here puzzled them. They shrugged and looked puzzled, but that may have been because no one in the Garcia family has been able to speak Spanish for three generations, including Dave.

All the dead babies from the Massacre of the Innocents are conveniently buried one grotto over, under the same church. Sites of Christian devotion around Jerusalem tend to be convenient. In the Church of the Holy Sepulcher the piece of ground where Christ's cross was erected, the stone where He was laid out for burial, and the tomb in which He was resurrected—plus where Adam's skull was buried and, according to early Christian cartographers, the center of the world—are within a few arthritic steps of one another. Saint Helena, the mother of the emperor Constantine, was over seventy-five when she traveled to the Holy Land, in 326 A.D., looking for sacred locations. Arriving with a full imperial retinue and a deep purse, Saint Helena discovered that her tour guides were able to take her to every place she wanted to go; each turned out to be nearby and, as luck would have it, for sale. The attack of real estate agents in Palestine long predates Zionism.

The Church of the Nativity is a shabby mess, a result of quarreling religious orders. The Greek Orthodox, Armenian

Orthodox, and Roman Catholic priests have staked out Nativity turf with the acrimonious precision of teenage brothers sharing a bedroom. A locked steel door prevents direct access from the Roman Catholic chapel to the Manger Grotto, which has to be reached through the Greek Orthodox monastery where there is a particular "Armenian beam" that Greek Orthodox monks stand on to sweep the area above the grotto entrance, making the Armenians so angry that, according to my guidebook, "in 1984 there were violent clashes as Greek and Armenian clergy fought running battles with staves and chains that had been hidden beneath their robes." What would Christ have thought? He might have thought, "Hand me a stave," per Mark 11:15: "Jesus went into the temple, and began to cast out them that sold and bought in the temple, and overthrew the tables of the moneychangers."

It's left to the Muslims to keep the peace at the Church of the Nativity in Bethlehem, just as it's left to the Jews to keep a similar peace at the likewise divided Church of the Holy Sepulcher in Jerusalem. Who will be a Muslim and a Jew to the Muslims and the Jews? Hindus, maybe. That is more or less the idea behind putting UN peacekeeping troops in Israel. This may or may not work. The *Bhagavad Gita* opens with the hero Arjuna trying to be a pacifist: "Woe!" Arjuna says. "We have resolved to commit a great crime as we stand ready to kill family out of greed for kingship and pleasures!" But the Lord Krishna tells Arjuna to quit whining and fight. "Either you are killed and will then attain to heaven," Krishna says, "or you triumph and will enjoy the earth."

Our guide took us to several large gift shops with no other customers, aisles stacked with unsold souvenirs of Jesus' birth. Part of the Israeli strategy in the intifada has been to put economic pressure on the Arabs of the West Bank and

Gaza. Fear of death hasn't stopped the Arabs. Maybe fear of Chapter 11 will do the trick. The hopes and fears of all the years reside with badly carved olive-wood crèche sets. Dave and I bought several.

Then our guide took us up a hill to the Christian Arab village of Beit Jala, which the Israelis had been shelling. Large chunks were gone from the tall, previously comfortable-looking limestone villas. Shuttered housefronts were full of what looked like bullet holes, but large enough to put a Popsicle in. "Ooh, fifty-caliber," said Dave with professional appreciation.

"These people," our guide said, "have no part in the violence." Dave and I made noises of condolence and agreement in that shift of sympathy to the nearest immediate victim that is the hallmark of twenty-first-century morality.

"Here a man was sleeping in his bed," said our guide, showing us a three-story pile of rubble. "And they couldn't find him for days later. The Israelis shell here for no reason."

"Um," said Dave, "*why* for no reason?" And our guide, speaking in diplomatic circumlocution, allowed as how every now and then, all the time, Palestinian gunmen would occasionally, very often, use the Beit Jala hilltop to shoot with rifles at Israeli tanks guarding a highway tunnel in the valley. They did it the next night.

"It's kind of a rule of military tactics," said Dave to me, sotto voce, as we walked back to the car, "not to shoot a rifle at a tank when the tank knows where you are." Unless, of course, scanty olive-wood-crèche-set sales are spoiling your enjoyment of earth and you've decided to attain to heaven.

The owner of an upscale antiquities store back in Bethlehem did not look as if he meant to attain any sooner than necessary, even though his store's air-conditioning unit had been knocked out by Israelis firing on nearby rioters. He arrived in a new Mercedes with three assistants to open his business especially for Dave, his first customer in a month.

The antiquities dealer was another friend of Z's. Z told us that this was the man whose grandfather was the Palestinian cobbler to whom the Dead Sea Scrolls were offered as scrap leather by the Bedouin shepherd who found them—a story too good to subject to the discourtesies of investigative journalism.

The emporium was new, built in the soon-dashed hopes of millennium traffic. The antiquities were displayed with the stark, track-lit modern exhibition drama necessary to make them look like something other than the pots and pans and jars and bottles from people who had, one way or another, given up on this place long ago.

Dave collects antiques, but by profession he's an iron and steel commodities trader. He has also lived in Asia for years. I sat on a pile of rugs and drank little cups of coffee while Levantine bargaining met Oriental dickering and the cold-eyed brokerage of the market floor. The three great world traditions of haggle flowered into confrontation for two and a half hours. Folks from the Oslo talks and the Camp David meetings should have been there for benefit of instruction. Everyone ended up happy. No fatal zero-sum thinking was displayed as banknotes and ceramics changed hands at last. Dave could make more money. And the Arabs could make more antiquities.

Why can't everybody just get along? No reasonably detached person goes to Israel without being reduced in philosophical discourse to the level of Rodney King—or, for that matter, to the level of George Santayana. "Those who cannot remember the past are condemned to repeat it," Santayana said in one of those moments of fatuousness that come to even the most detached of philosophers. In Israel and Palestine, as in Serbia and Kosovo, this goes double for those who can't remember anything else. And everybody *does* get along, after a fashion. Muslims and Christians and Jews have lived together in the Holy Land for centuries—hating one another's guts, cutting one another's throats, and touching off wars of various magnitudes.

The whole melodrama of the Middle East would be improved if amnesia were as common here as it is in the plots of imaginary melodramas. I was thinking this as I was looking at the Dead Sea Scrolls in the solemn underground Shrine of the Book, inside the vast precincts of the Israel Museum. Maybe, I thought, all the world's hoary old tracts ought to wind up as loafer soles or be auctioned at Sotheby's to a greedy high-tech billionaire for display in his otherwise bookless four-thousand-square-foot cyber-den. Then I noticed that Z was reading the scrolls, muttering aloud at speed, perusing an ancient text with more ease than I can read Henry James. What's past is past, perhaps, but when it passed, this was where it went.

Z dropped us at the King David Hotel, the headquarters of the Palestinian mandate administration when the British were trying to keep the peace. In 1946 the hotel was blown up by the radical wing of the Jewish Resistance Movement, the Irgun. Some of every group were killed—forty-one Arabs, twenty-eight British, seventeen Jews, and five reasonably detached persons of miscellaneous designation. The Irgun was led by the future prime minister Menachem Begin, who would make peace with Egypt in the 1970s but, then again, war with Lebanon in the 1980s.

On the way to the hotel Z explained why there will always be war in the region. "Israel is strategic," he said in his most New Testamental tone. "It is the strategic land bridge between Africa and Asia. For five thousand years there has been fighting in Israel. It is the strategic land bridge." And the fighting continues, a sort of geopolitical muscle memory, as though airplanes and supertankers hadn't been invented. The English and the French might as well be fighting over the beaver-pelt trade in Quebec today, and from what I understand of Canadian politics, they are.

We were meeting Israeli friends of Dave's at the hotel, a married couple. He voted for Sharon; she voted for Ehud Barak. Dave and I marked our lintels and doorposts with the blood of the lamb, metaphorically speaking, and drank Israeli vodka and orange juice.

"There will always be war," the husband said, "because with war Arafat is a hero and without war he's just an unimportant guy in charge of an unimportant place with a lot of political and economic problems."

"There will always be war," the wife said, "because with war Sharon is a hero and without war he's just an unimportant guy in charge of an unimportant place with . . ."

Also, war is fun—from a distance. Late the next night Dave and I were walking back to our hotel in Arab East Jerusalem. Dave was wearing a Hawaiian shirt and I was in a blazer and chinos. We couldn't have looked less Israeli if we'd been dressed like Lawrence of Arabia (who, incidentally, was a third party to the cordial meeting between Chaim Weizmann and the emir Faisal). Fifty yards down a side street a couple of Palestinian teenagers jumped out of the shadows. Using the girlie overhand throw of nations that mostly play soccer, one kid threw a bottle at us. It landed forty yards away.

On Good Friday, Dave and Z and I walked from the Garden of Gethsemane to the Lions Gate, where Israeli paratroopers fought their way into the Old City during the Six-Day War. We traveled the Via Dolorosa in an uncrowded quiet that Jesus Christ and those paratroopers were not able to enjoy. We owed our peace in Jerusalem to an enormous police presence. This did Jesus no good. Nor did the Jordanian police give Israeli soldiers helpful directions to the Ecce Homo Arch. And our Savior and the heroes of 1967 didn't have a chance to stop along the way and bargain with Arab rug merchants.

Z and the rug merchants exchanged pessimisms, Z grousing about Sharon and the Arabs complaining about Arafat. "The Israeli army tells Arafat where the strikes will come," one shopkeeper said. "They tell him, 'Don't be here. Don't be there.' No one tells me."

I visited the fourteen Stations of the Cross and said my prayers, for peace, of course, although, as a Zionist friend of mine puts it, "Victory would be okay, too." Jesus said, "Love your enemies." He didn't say not to have any. In fact, He said, "I came not to send peace but a sword." Or, anyway, staves and chains.

Then we went to the Wailing Wall, the remnant of the Second Temple, built by the same Herod the Great who killed all the babies buried by the manger in Bethlehem. Atop the Wailing Wall stands the Haram al Sharif, with the Dome of the Rock enclosing Mount Moriah, where Abraham was ready to kill Isaac and where, at that moment, Muslims gathered for Friday prayers were surrounded by Israeli soldiers, some of both no doubt also ready to kill. (The Dome of the Rock marks the center of the world for those who don't believe that the center of the world is down the street, in the Church of the Holy Sepulcher.)

In the plaza in front of the Wailing Wall religious volunteers were lending yarmulkes to Jews who had arrived bareheaded. "Well," Dave said, "my mother was Jewish, so I guess that makes me Jewish. I'd better get a rent-a-beanie and go over to the Wailing Wall and . . . wail, or something."

The yarmulkes being handed out were, unaccountably, made of silver reflective fabric. "I look like an outer-space Jew," Dave said.

"I always thought you were Catholic," I said.

"Because of *Garcia*," Dave said, "like *O'Rourke*."

I said, "But I'm not Catholic, either. My mother was Presbyterian, and I'm Methodist. I came home from Methodist confirmation class in a big huff and told my mother there were huge differences between Presbyterians and Methodists. And my mother said, 'We sent you to the Methodist church because all the nice people in the neighborhood go there.'"

"They could use that church here," Dave said.

Dave swayed in front of the wall like the Orthodox surrounding him, although, frankly, in a manner more aging-pop-fan than Hassidic.

What could cause more hatred and bloodshed than religion? This is the Israel question. Except it isn't rhetorical; it has an answer. We went to Yad Vashem, the Jerusalem Holocaust Memorial, and saw what the godless get up to.

There are worse things than war, if the intifada is indeed a war. As of May 2001, 513 Palestinians and 124 Israelis had been killed in what is called the second intifada. About 40,000 perished in the 1992–1996 civil war in Tajikistan that nobody's heard of. From 1.5 to 2 million are dead in Sudan. There are parts of the world where the situation Dave and I were in is too ordinary to have a name.

Late Saturday night the particular place where we were in that situation was the American Colony Hotel, in East Jerusalem, sometimes called the "PLO Hotel" for the supposed connections the staff has. It is the preferred residence of intifada-covering journalists, especially those who are indignant about Israeli behavior. The American Colony Hotel was once the mansion of an Ottoman pasha. Dave and I sat among palms in the peristyle courtyard, surrounded by arabesques carved in Jerusalem's golden limestone. The bedroom-temperature air was scented with Easter lilies and in the distance, now and then, gunfire could be heard.

"This country is hopeless," Dave said, pouring a Palestinian Taybeh beer to complement a number of Israeli Maccabee beers we'd had earlier in West Jerusalem. "And as hopeless places go, it's not bad." We discussed another Israel question. Why are Israeli girls so fetching in their army uniforms? It may have something to do with their carrying guns. But Freud was a lukewarm Zionist and let's not think about it.

After the first Zionist Congress, in 1897, the rabbis of Vienna sent a delegation to Palestine on a fact-finding mission. The delegation cabled Vienna, saying, "The bride is beautiful, but she is married to another man." However, the twentieth century, with all its Freudianism, was about to dawn, and we know what having the beautiful bride married to another man means in today's melodramas. No fair using amnesia as a device for tidy plot resolution.

"Do we have to choose sides?" Dave said. But it's like dating sisters. Better make a decision or head for the Global Village limits. And speaking of sisters, I opened *The Jerusalem Post* on Easter morning and discovered that my sister's neighborhood in Cincinnati was under curfew, overrun with race riots.

4

9/11 DIARY

SEPTEMBER 11, 2001

When the Pentagon was hit, Debbie Lehan, the manager of my apartment building in Washington, D.C., and Damon Boone, the building engineer, moved their cars out of the underground garage and parked them to block both ends of the building's horseshoe drive. Of course that was absurd—as if the terrorists had thought, "World Trade Center, Pentagon, and . . . the place on Connecticut Avenue where Naomi Wolf used to live." But by noon all the building's children had been gathered home from school or day care. The children played in the empty half-oval. Career daddies and career mommies hovered. The barricaded driveway was absurd, if you could keep your eyes from misting.

"Better to do *something*," Debbie said.

Damon unlocked the door to the building's roof. We could see the Pentagon on fire across the Potomac. "It makes me angry, scared, sad all at once," said Damon. According to the theory of terrorism, it was supposed to make him paralyzed with terror.

The traffic on Connecticut Avenue was coming from downtown as if in the evening rush hour. But there was none of the accustomed honking at the District's unsequenced and haphazardly placed stoplights.

Downtown the cars were gone and the stores were closed. Police officers stood in ones and twos. On the corner of F and Fourteenth streets two businessmen, two messengers, and a panhandler were listening to the panhandler's portable radio. A tape of President Bush's first response to the terrorist attack was being broadcast. One of the messengers said, in the voice people use when they're saying something important, "After today things will never be the same." Then he seemed to have one of those moments that came to everyone on September 11, with jumbled thoughts alike in size but wildly mismatched in weight—pity, rage, and how to get the shirts back from the dry cleaner. "Transportation in the air won't be as fast," he said, in a smaller voice.

At the corner of Fourteenth and Constitution a policeman set out flares to block the street. The policeman took the plastic caps off the flares and tossed the caps aside with the decisive gesture of a man suspending minor public mores in a crisis. A young man on a bicycle stopped at the curb and said to me, "At least the grocery stores are open. But the trucks can't get to the stores. If it's going to be a big international war, I'll just fast."

The young man had a theory that the terrorism had to do with America's pulling out of the UN conference on racism in South Africa, but he was interrupted by a woman indignant that the portable toilets at the Washington Monument were still in use. "They don't know *what* I could be doing in there," she said.

The grass expanse in the middle of the Mall was deserted except for the homeless, suddenly homeless alone. Like everyone else, they seemed subdued, although they didn't stay subdued. The next day, at Eighteenth and L, I would see a ragged man in the middle of the street shouting, "I'll kill all of you people! I don't like any of you!" No one, including the soldiers who were by then everywhere in Washington, paid attention.

Michele Lieber, a lobbyist who lives in my building, had come downtown with me. Alongside the Mall, snack and souvenir trucks were dutifully open. Michele asked a snack-truck proprietor if business was good. "Yes, of course," he dutifully said.

That day, for the first time in thirteen years in Washington, I saw no protesters. And hardly any were around on Wednesday. A reopened Lafayette Park would feature only an old woman with a sign saying WHITE HOUSE ANTI-NUCLEAR PEACE VIGIL SINCE 1981 and a middle-aged hippie on a similar anti-nuclear sleep-out SINCE 1984. The old woman was talking mostly to herself. "They provoked what happened," she said. The hippie was talking to two adolescent girls with piercings, discussing his pet squirrel.

On Tuesday afternoon even TV crews were mostly absent from the White House vicinity. On Constitution at the Ellipse, ABC White House correspondent Terry Moran was on a lone stand-up, not saying much to the camera. A few people gathered around. "We just got here from Slovakia and everything happened," a tourist said.

Michele and I had walked to the reflecting pool behind the Capitol before we saw any more tourists. A family in sport clothes was standing there looking baffled. I introduced myself to the father, and his first words were (one is grateful for not having a conspiratorial turn of mind), "We're from Slovakia."

"We are a bit concerned," the father said, "but the weather is okay. We had only one day to be here. Tomorrow we are supposed to go to New York."

Michele, on her cell phone, was trying to call friends in New York. She kept getting a recorded message, "Due to the tornado your call cannot go through."

At Bullfeathers, a restaurant on First Street, Representative Don Sherwood, Republican from the Tenth District in Pennsylvania, was having lunch with his daughter. He wanted a session of Congress to be convened at the Capitol that night. "We should be as visible and in-business as possible," he said.

Four or five televisions were on inside the restaurant, their volume turned up. Another congressman and his female aide were in the men's room, the only place quiet enough for the congressman to do a phone interview. The congressman was saying, "We will make the people who did this pay. It is awfully hard to defend yourself from people who have no respect for human life." He seemed to be pulling in two directions—as did the soldiers on the streets the next day, camouflaged for invisibility and wearing blaze-orange traffic control vests.

"We just have to quit being Americans for a little while," said a staffer from the Republican National Committee. "Forget about carrying our constitution to people who don't give a rat's ass."

Michele and I walked across Capitol Hill. On Massachusetts we met a Senate staffer whom Michele knew. He was jogging. "It was a little hairy when they told us to evacuate," he said. "Then I saw our F-16s fly over, and I felt okay."

We met another Senate staffer who was trying to get his car out of a parking lot that was inside the police cordon around the Capitol. The four of us walked to the Dubliner bar on North Capital Street.

"The congressional leadership," said the second staffer, "has been whisked off to 'an undisclosed location.' As far as I'm concerned they can keep most of them there." This touched on another theory of terrorism: that the organization of society can be attacked by striking at organizations; that we can't organize things ourselves.

"Four Guinness," the first Senate staffer said to the bartender.

"Time to take sides," the second staffer said.

"Time to turn sand into glass," said the first.

Ariel Sharon was on CNN. "It is a war between the good and the bad," said Sharon.

From the Dubliner we took a cab to the Palm restaurant on Nineteenth Street. The bar and the dining room were full. President Bush came on television at 8:30. Everyone has seen, in movies, a restaurant go quiet. I had never before really heard all talk come to a halt and all noise from tableware cease. The customers and staff applauded when the president said, "We will make no distinction between the people who committed these acts and the people who harbor them."

"As I was driving in to open for lunch," the Palm's assistant general manager, Jocelyn Zarr, said, "all the traffic was going the other way. Ten minutes after the Pentagon was hit, I was getting reservations. I'm thinking, 'Aren't these people watching the news?' But they were. They just wanted to be with other people. I told the staff that if anyone wanted to go home, just go. No one did. I opened early. People were streaming in. My only fear was putting a group of people in danger. Once I got past that, I thought, 'The Palm is the center point.' Everyone wanted to come and sit at the bar and talk. Smith and Wollensky called and asked what I was going to do. I said I was staying open. All the evening staff showed up. A friend called and said, 'You shouldn't be working when thousands of people died.' But what else am I going to do?"

On Monday night, September 10, I had finished an article for *The Atlantic* about Israel (an article that appears as the previous chapter in this book). Israel is a country that has been under terrorist attack for generations, forever. On Tuesday I didn't want to publish the article. It wasn't serious enough. I was thinking "After today things will never be the same." Lines from W. H. Auden's poem "September 1, 1939" kept coming to mind:

> *Waves of anger and fear*
> *Circulate over the bright*
> *And darkened lands of the earth*

By Wednesday I realized I'd never known what Auden was getting at with that poem, except, perhaps, in "As the

clever hopes expire / Of a low dishonest decade." Apt enough,
but . . .

> *Where blind skyscrapers use*
> *Their full height to proclaim*
> *The strength of Collective Man*

What's that crap? Or this:

> *Ironic points of light*
> *Flash out whenever the Just*
> *Exchange their messages*

Anyway, Auden repudiated the poem, mostly because
of the fatuous line "We must love one another or die." Or
just die. And neither agape nor eros is an appropriate response to Osama bin Laden. Also, Auden was the English-
man who, when World War II loomed, acted as Hitler would
have had Englishmen act—he ran to America and stayed there.
In Israel, on September 11, things were the same as ever.

SEPTEMBER 30, 2001

Traveling to London from Washington twelve days after the
terrorist attack, I expected security measures. I'd been told
to arrive at Dulles Airport three hours before departure. I was
ready for checkpoints where people in flak jackets would use
mirrors to look for bombs under cars—although, nowadays,
with automotive electronics and the puzzle plumbing of emissions control, everything under cars looks like a bomb.
Anyway, the checkpoints weren't there.

At the ticket counter, instead of being asked once,
"Hasyourluggagebeenunderyourcontrolatalltimes," I was

asked twice. The metal detectors and X-ray machines were operated by the usual dim but friendly minimum-wage security guards, now somewhat less friendly. I was told to hand over my disposable lighter, to prevent, I suppose, any threat of "Do what I say or I'll light this Marlboro and you'll all die— in thirty years due to inhalation of secondhand smoke."

I headed cheerlessly to the designated smoking area, expecting to find a roomful of desperate, fireless people paying black-market prices for Nicorette. Everyone was smoking. I asked for a light, and someone produced a disposable lighter. It seems that if you went through one of the airport's two security portals, you were made to surrender all lighters and matches. But if you went through the other . . .

Concern had been voiced that fear of terrorism could lead to renewed racial profiling. Never mind that the languages of the Taliban—Pashto and Dari—are part of the Indo-European linguistic family and that, if "Caucasian" has any meaning at all, Afghans have a better claim to it than Hungarians or Finns.

The profiling at the boarding gate couldn't be called racial, exactly. The ruddy and the pallid were ushered directly on board, as were the sufficiently black. It was the tanned or swarthy who had to line up for additional questioning. On my flight these included, as far as I could tell, some Hindus, some Filipinos, a Hispanic or two, and a pair of elderly Iranian women wearing chadors in violation of the new American no-unusual-things-on-your-head taboo that has brought grief to Sikhs in the U.S. hinterland. (Not that there hasn't been Sikh terrorism, but it was directed against Indira Gandhi, in retaliation for the Indian army's storming the Golden Temple at Amritsar. This isn't an issue at the mo-

ment, but the complexities of building an international coalition against terrorism could lead to India demanding a wholesale revocation of Sikh cab licenses in New York, thereby
bringing that city to a halt again.)

An English friend asked me, "Would a bald chap who
was sunburned and was gardening and put a tea towel on
his head be in trouble in America?"

My plane was two thirds empty. But the unflappable
British flight crew was unflapped. I was not subjected to the
indignity that an acquaintance suffered on a flight from New
York to Chicago. He was made to press the flight attendant
call button and identify himself before being allowed to go
to the bathroom. This—for a drinking man in the enlarged-
prostate years—is a serious violation of civil rights.

The people I know in Great Britain were in the same state of
shock and anger as the people I know in America. And, like
my American friends, they weren't particularly frightened of
a second terrorist strike or of poison gas or germ warfare. But
this may be a matter of being old smokers and drinkers, of
an age for cardiac arrest and malignancy, with children they'd
like to see grow up or at least get a damn job, and retirement
funds that had gone to hell during the previous year. How
much more frightening can life get?

The Brits, however, were more likely to raise the subject of the IRA and say a word about America leading the
fight against terrorism while letting the NORAID cans be
passed in the bars of Southie and the Bronx. I blamed the
Kennedys—always a safe course when questions of bad U.S.
political policies are raised. Meanwhile, it's the British

themselves who were at the negotiating table with my moron cousins from Ulster. Personally, I'd start the war on terrorism with Gerry Adams. At least we know where he is.

Incidentally, it's ridiculous if you're Irish to claim that you can't fathom the mind-set behind the wild destruction of innocents, the casual self-murder, and the bathos of martyrdom on September 11. Al Qaeda probably has a Yeats of its own—"A terrible beauty is born."

But there was something going on in Great Britain, among the people I *don't* know, that was more troubling than Northern Ireland home-rule concessions. The September 17 issue of *The New Statesman* ran an amazing editorial leader:

> Look at the pictures on pages 6–7, showing Americans running in terror from the New York explosions and then ask yourself how often in the past (particularly in Vietnam and more recently in Iraq) you have seen people running in terror from American firepower. American bond traders, you may say, are as innocent and as undeserving of terror as Vietnamese or Iraqi peasants. Well, yes and no.

To quote more might set off a wave of retribution in America against people wearing derby hats.

I had dinner with the critic and television commentator Clive James and his assistant. The assistant was an able and well-educated young woman who could not be convinced by Clive that, in the matter of moral values, there was such a thing as a superior culture. "They cover their women in the ballroom drapes!" Clive said. "Your dad can have you stoned to death for not marrying some old goat!"

"I wouldn't call it an inferior culture," his assistant said.

"What about Somalia?! What about clitoridectomies?!"

"Of course I'm a feminist," his assistant said. "But I resist the idea of an inferior culture."

It's usually Clive and I who have the arguments. He's a liberal democrat. But he's my age; he remembers when the whole point of being on the left was the effort (alas, misplaced) to forge a superior culture.

I was a guest on a BBC radio phone-in talk show. If the world is mad at America for anything, it should be for invention of the phone-in talk show. The idea of a news broadcast once was to find someone with information and broadcast it. The idea now is to find someone with ignorance and spread it around. (Being ignorant myself, I'm not mad personally.)

A woman named Rhona called and said we didn't have enough empathy for the poor people in the world. We're so rich and they're so poor, no wonder they're angry.

I told her that was a slur on poor people. And anyway, Osama bin Laden is a rich twit.

Rhona said that we are so wealthy and materialistic and they are so deprived. "Here I am," she said, "just an ordinary suburban housewife in a semidetached, and I'm surrounded by all these things I don't need." Privately I was thinking that my moron cousins from Belfast could fix that with breaking and entering. I said, "You're arguing completely beside the point." She was employing a fallacy of relevance, specifically what's called in logic *argumentum ad misericordiam* (although I had to look that up later; what I said on the radio was "So what?").

Rhona accused me of that most grievous of contemporary sins, especially when committed against a woman by a middle-aged man. "Don't patronize me," she said.

Calls and e-mails were nine to one in Rhona's favor, but one stalwart sent this message: "I suspect why ninety percent of callers are not in favor of P.J.'s opinions is because they are out-of-work socialists who have nothing better to do but phone radio stations."

And there are some of their ilk in the United States. Back in Washington, I went to a peace rally on September 29 at Freedom Plaza, near the White House. Several thousand people attended. As I arrived, a man on the speaker's platform was saying, "We cannot permit the president of our country to claim there are only two forces—good and evil. We are not with either."

The Bread and Puppet Theater troupe was carrying a score of what appeared to be eight-foot-high papiermâché baked potatoes. Asked what this was about, one of the troupe said it represented "naked people being oppressed by clothed people." Asked again, she said the same thing.

Members of another performing arts group were wearing cardboard bird heads and flapping bedsheets. They said they were "the cranes of peace."

A woman asked for signatures on a petition in favor of affirmative action. The National Youth Rights Association had set up a card table with a sign reading LOWER THE DRINKING AGE. Snappy protest rhymes seemed as yet inchoate. Drumming and pogo dancing accompanied the chant "Stop the war / In Afganistan / While we / Still can!"

Another speaker came to the podium and said, "Let us bomb the world with housing." One of those McMansions with the lawyer foyer and the cathedral-ceilinged great room could do real damage.

Vegetarian demonstrators carried large banners illustrated with vegetables. A carrot was captioned "Intelligence." Placards in the crowd read KILLING IS BAD; POVERTY IS TERRIBLE TOO; ABOLISH MONEY FOR A WORLD OF SHARING; and CONGRESS PLEASE KEEP A COOL HEAD. One young man wore a headband scrawled with VICTORY 4 CHECHNYA. Another carried a black-and-red ensign that he said stood for "anarchosyndicalism," a word I didn't think had been spoken aloud since *Monty Python and the Holy Grail.* "Do you work for the police?" the standard-bearer asked. My work-shirt-and-chinos liberal disguise was ineffective.

A child of nine or ten, wearing a FUCK WAR T-shirt, harangued some police officers. The officers could not keep straight faces. Most of the other demonstrators were of college age with subdermal ink, transdermal hardware, and haircuts from the barber college on Mars. But people my age were present, too, and beginning to resemble Bertrand Russell, especially the women. Then I saw him: a hippie with a walker, wearing a hearing aid. Sic transit generation gap.

Demonstrators tried to burn an American flag. They had trouble lighting it. Maybe their matches had been taken by airport security—or maybe all the antismoking propaganda aimed at the young has come home to roost in a lack of fire-making skills. When the flag at last caught flame, a passerby shoved his way into the crowd. He was a normal-looking man without great height or bulk. He began to throw punches. He was set upon by twenty-five or thirty of the . . . anarchosyndicalists, I guess. There was a momentary geyser of funny clothes, odd hairstyles, and flopping tattooed limbs. The normal-looking man emerged, slightly winded, carrying the remains of the flag and having received a small scuff on the forehead.

OCTOBER 21, 2001

Six weeks into the War on Terrorism, contemporary war seemed to exhibit the vulgarity that Oscar Wilde said would be needed to make warfare unpopular. That is to say, the opening offensive of this war was directed at the quotidian, the workaday, the commonplace, the vulgar—ordinary people working at their daily jobs in office buildings. And common people, not self-exalted jihad warriors, were showing the bravery and making the sacrifices in Afghanistan as well as the United States. Then, in a more Wildean sense of the world "vulgar," there came the anthrax contamination. A cowflop of a weapon elicited all sorts of bull in response. On October 20 the *Los Angeles Times* devoted 465 column inches to a disease that had sickened fewer people than the corporation that makes the antibiotic by which the disease is cured. Only a few months before, Bayer had withdrawn the anticholesterol drug Baycol after it had been linked to fifty-two deaths.

Fortunately, my family doctor, William Hughes, has expertise in the most virulent aspect of anthrax—publicity. Dr. Hughes is married to ABC White House correspondent Ann Compton. He suggested that I get a ciprofloxacin prescription, lest anyone think I was too low in the journalism hierarchy to receive threatening mail. And indeed there were threats in my mail, but only the usual ones from Visa, American Express, and the landlord.

One of the first anthrax attacks was made against the company that owns *The National Enquirer*. The company's name is displayed in large letters on its suburban Florida offices: AMERICAN MEDIA. Supposing that the anthrax contamination is really the work of terrorists, al Qaeda may be less sophisticated than we feared. "Ah," thought the bin Laden operatives, "*here* is where the American media have their place of headquarters." On the other hand, considering the role of supermarket tabloids in America's life of the mind, al Qaeda may be more sophisticated than we thought.

Anyway, the media were enormously reassuring, simultaneously telling the public that members of the public won't contract anthrax while giving nonstop coverage to the members of the public who did, will, or might. Then Tom Ridge, the head of the Office of Homeland Security, came on the air, reminding us how much "Homeland Security" sounds like a failed savings-and-loan. Didn't Grandma lose $15,000 in a CD when Homeland Security went under? The media also recounted the complete list of symptoms for all three types of anthrax infection—symptoms that correspond to those of the common cold, the flu, a hangover, acne, and eating the church-picnic potato salad.

According to CNN on October 19, being infected with the intestinal form of anthrax results in "nausea, lack of appetite, and fever." And—if boiling rage counts as fever—so did being on a commercial flight. I had flown on ten during the five weeks after September 11, owing to an author tour for a badly timed collection of light humorous essays. (Not that I'm complaining about being knocked off the medium-well-seller list by people who spent five minutes with Osama bin Laden's brother-in-law in 1976. Especially not after hearing publishing-world scuttlebutt about a certain Manhattan novelist famous for tales of fashion models and drug excess, whose reaction on September 11, it's said, was to exclaim how glad he was that he didn't have a book out. Discriminating readers are *always* glad when he doesn't have a book out.)

Airport security would soon be turned over to the government so that a federal agency could do the same fine job of protecting the nation in the future that the CIA and the FBI did in early September. Meanwhile, "heightened security precautions" were allowing airlines to perfect their technique of treating passengers like convicted felons and providing all the transportation amenities usually accorded to smuggled cockatoos.

At the Los Angeles airport I watched as an elderly, arthritic man was forced to remove his buckle shoes and send them through the carry-on baggage X ray. In Ontario, California, a friend was meeting me at the airport. Of course he couldn't wait at curbside. He had to circle through the arrivals lane while slugs (slugs with valid photo IDs!) delivered my checked bags. On the forth go-round a policeman stepped into the road and told my friend that if he drove by one more time he'd be arrested.

What caused the giant python lines at airport security checkpoints remained a mystery. An acquaintance, a plastic surgeon who specializes in cranial reconstruction, was returning from a conference on head injuries shortly after September 11. His hand luggage contained three human skulls. These passed unnoticed through the X-ray screening.

Doubtless all sorts of civil rights must be sacrificed temporarily in times of crisis. But there is no ACLU for comfort and convenience. A generation hence we'll be living in a world of metal detectors in nudist colonies.

Traveling around the country did, however, allow me to see how different regions of America were coping with current events. On October 9 a local TV anchorman in Washington, D.C., called Islam (using an adjective perhaps left behind by the sudden journalistic shift away from celebrity obsession) "the second most popular religion on earth." It has an amazing Q factor, too, that Islam.

At about the same time, aided by the Internet, there was a cheerful realization nationwide that "Taliban" scans perfectly in "The Banana Boat Song":

> Come Mr. Taliban, rid me of Osama.
> Air Force come and it flatten me home.
>> Cruise missile,
>> Tomahawk,
>> Half-ton bomb.
> Air Force come and it flatten me home.

On October 16, in Austin, Texas, local TV reported that the Austin fire department had responded to a call from a household concerning a "suspicious package." The sole suspicious thing about the package was that it had been mailed from New York City.

On October 19 a chipper announcer for KFWB radio, in southern California, said, "Anthrax news certainly has Orange County people talking . . ." Later that day, at a lunch in Simi Valley, I was sitting next to someone from the Ventura County district attorney's office. He said anthrax alarms were coming in at a rate of one every three minutes, and that the only practical decontamination response would be to have people get naked and be hosed down. That evening, on the set of a public-television book show, T. C. Boyle talked about how he had a certain admiration for acts of "ecotage," but in his fiction he tried to show both sides of the story. He managed never to mention September 11.

I can remember when powdery white substances of sinister origin were doing a lot more damage to America than anthrax had done so far. Circa 1980 America's elite was suffering "nasaltage." It emptied bank accounts, wrecked marriages, ruined thousands of careers, and brought the nation to its knees (with a soda straw over a glass coffee table). But Attorney General John Ashcroft was very firm in stating that anthrax threats are no laughing matter. Pranks and jests concerning anthrax would be treated as serious criminal actions. Thus various larval jokes with "You've got mail" punch lines had to be allowed to die before maturation. And the heavy-metal band Anthrax was said to be considering changing its name—presumably to Chicken Pox.

Were we as a nation forgetting what our international critics have been saying about us for years? Aren't we supposed to be a big, terrifying country, a Godzilla of capitalism wrecking the globe? Since when did Godzilla flip out because he might have brushed against something in the mail room while he was devouring Trenton, New Jersey? Since when did Godzilla turn (devastating) tail and scamper to Mexico to buy Cipro over the counter? I trusted this was a momentary lapse. And I hoped that Osama bin Laden was discovering, amid smart bombs and Delta Forces in Afghanistan, that America isn't scared, America is *scary*. The members of al Qaeda had gotten dressed up in their holy-warrior costumes and gone trick-or-treating at the wrong house.

NOVEMBER 26, 2001

Lo! The intrepid Afghan Taliban fighter of warrior lineage ancient. He who had vanquished countless foes, unassailable in his mountain redoubts, imbued with fanatical resolve, possessed by suicidal courage—and who was now running around Mazar-e-Sharif getting his beard shaved, playing Uzbecki pop music on his boom box, and using Mrs. Afghan Warrior's burka for a bedspread in the guest room, soon to be rented to foreign aid workers.

The fighting in Afghanistan was so brief that CNN Headline News had to delete three bars from its "Target: Terror" score to keep the theme music from outlasting the hostilities. The Soviet Union fought the Afghans for ten years and gave up in ignominious defeat in 1989. What were the Soviets using for weapons—cafeteria buns and rolled-up locker room towels? The United States dropped a lot of cafeteria buns—or emergency food aid that is very like cafeteria buns—on Taliban-controlled areas. Exposure to American school-lunch fare may have been the deciding factor in the radical Muslim demoralization. A country that can make something that dreadful from mere flour, yeast, and water is a country not to be defied.

However it was that we achieved victory, achieve it we did, although to what end remains to be seen. One effect of victory (though very temporary) was to make America's elite even more sanguine about armed conflict than they had been during the 1999 air war on Serbia. SURPRISE: WAR WORKS AFTER ALL, read the headline on the Week in Review section of *The New York Times* for Sunday, November 18, 2001. That same day *The Boston Globe Magazine* ran a cover story titled "The New Patriots: College students support a country at war—and so do their Vietnam-era parents." Of course, there was the possibility that the revived fighting spirit among America's elite had nothing to do with Afghanistan but was a collateral result of Harvard's first undefeated football season since 1913. I believe Harvard played Mount Holyoke, Smith, Li'l Dickens Day Care Center, and several Pop Warner League teams, but I didn't check that.

Meanwhile, what next for our nation? Would we do, after the Afghan war, as we did after the Gulf War and just go home, have a recession, and elect some creepy Democratic governor of an obscure state as the next president? Or would we finish the War on Terrorism? The U.S. Department of State publication *Patterns of Global Terrorism 2000* seemed to offer ample opportunities for pursuing the latter goal:

> Iran remained the most active state sponsor of terrorism. . . . It provided increasing support to numerous terrorist groups, including the Lebanese Hizballah, HAMAS, and the Palestine Islamic Jihad (PIJ). . . . Iraq continued to serve as a safe haven and support to a variety of Palestinian rejectionist groups. . . . Syria continued to provide safehaven and support to several terrorist groups. . . . Sudan continued to serve as a safehaven for members of al-Qaida, the Lebanese Hizballah. . . . Egyptian Islamic Jihad, the PIJ, and HAMAS. . . .

We mustn't forget that this was not a war between Western civilization and the Muslim world. *The Washington Post* certainly hadn't forgotten. The *Post* made absolutely no comment about the real or apparent ethnicity of the person quoted in the following item about anthrax, which ran in the *Post*'s November 1, 2001, issue:

> "In hindsight, this has been an escalating event," said Mohammad Akhter, executive director of the American Public Health Association. "We will continue to see new cases of anthrax disease."

I was proud of *The Washington Post* and meant to write a complimentary letter to the editor, but I was too busy phoning in my tip to the FBI.

This was not a war between Western civilization and the Muslim world. There was, nonetheless, interesting reading to be done in *Freedom in the World,* a survey of political rights and civil liberties issued annually since 1955 by the nonpartisan organization Freedom House. Among countries whose populations are predominately (60 percent or more) Muslim, only remote Mali and tiny Benin were rated as "Free." On a scale of 1 (Canada) to 7 (god-awful), no other Muslim country received a score better than 3 in political rights and 4 in civil liberties.

Would we have to fight all those countries? Or could we just give them a hug? A peace vigil was being held each Saturday at noon outside the town offices in Peterborough, New Hampshire, a few miles from the house we own there.

According to the November 15, 2001, edition of the local newspaper, the *Monadnock Ledger,* "One week, when it was rumored that CBS might cover the protestors, 45 people showed up." By Saturday, November 17, the peace protest had, in effect, turned into a victory protest, and eight people were present. There was one sweet-faced, white-haired old lady, and then another who was so much older that she looked as if she might have been doing this sort of thing since the Hitler-Stalin Pact. There was a middle-aged man with hair that was both very long and gone from the top half of his head, a middle-aged woman upon whose features smugness had made an extensive and permanent settlement, a young man whose devil-may-care sideburns clashed with his go-to-hell golf pants, and a tweedy professor type who spent the whole vigil reading *The Nation.* Plus there was a mom in hand-knits trying to keep an eye on a rapidly fidgeting eight-year-old, and an Asian woman of college age who carried a sign reading RETALIATE WITH WORLD PEACE. Considering how world peace has gone for people in many places since the end of the Cold War, that's a harsh sentiment. After a while, the Asian woman wandered off to window-shop.

Most local New Englanders were ignoring the vigil with the perfect obliviousness to all incongruity that has been a New England hallmark since Henry David Thoreau went off to live a hermit's life at Walden Pond but continued to have his mother do his laundry. Only one fellow, flannel-clad, stopped to argue with the pacifists. "What do you do," the fellow asked, "when they strike the homeland? What if they roll right in here with tanks?" I was about to think "Good for you" when the fellow went on to say, "But I'll tell you one thing, I've refused to get the anthrax shots they're trying to give everybody."

So we see at what level debate about a just war and the natural right of self-defense was being conducted. The next morning, in a further sign of the times, Boston's WBZ Radio played a recorded segment by Martha Stewart detailing the intricacies of flag etiquette. The *New York Times* Sunday Styles section could not resist a bow to the New Seriousness—or an Afghanistan hook—even when reviewing the stupidest possible television show:

> First, network news programs broadcast images of Afghan women removing their burkas. . . . A few hours later . . . models had peeled away their clothing and were showing off thong panties as ABC broadcast the Victoria's Secret fashion show. . . .

And the November 20, 2001, issue of *The National Enquirer* had a feature headed "EVEN PETS ARE STRESSED

OUT FROM TERRORIST ATTACKS." Here are some of the signs that your dog, cat, or hamster was suffering from the aftereffects of 9/11:

• Sadness or glumness.
• Constant fighting with other pets.
• Lapses in toilet training.
• Pet is more needy and constantly seeks attention.

Speaking of constantly seeking attention, Bill Clinton showed up to give a talk at Harvard on November 19, perhaps to share anecdotes about his being a star quarterback on the undefeated Crimson gridiron squad of warrior linage ancient. *The Boston Globe* didn't mention his football heroics but did give Bill two fulsome stories and a teaser: "Fans flock to Clinton in Hub visit." According to the *Globe,* Bill "blamed himself for not building stronger ties with the Muslim world during the 1990's. . . . He said he should have worked harder . . . to support overseas 'nation building.'" In those days of flux and transformation there was comfort in knowing that some things stayed the same. It was still all about Bill. "America can exert influence, he said, by admitting its own faults." Interesting source for that advice. "We cannot engage in this debate," Bill was quoted as saying, "without admitting that there are excesses in our contemporary culture." Whether the ex-president was referring to himself or to the Victoria's Secret fashion show was not made clear.

During a question-and-answer period Clinton said that he supported the creation of a Palestinian state. It's a good idea. Islamic fundamentalists will need someplace to go.

Having them all in the West Bank and the Gaza Strip would allow the War on Terror to be conducted in a compact area with well-mapped terrain and an excellent road system. As long as the Israelis don't get involved. We wouldn't want anybody on our side who was guilty of premature antiterrorism.

5

EGYPT

December 2001

Hatred between Palestinians and Israelis abides. Arab-led Islamic fundamentalism destabilizes nations from Algeria to the Philippines. The threat of terrorist attacks by al Qaeda continues. Also, our cars need gas. It is important to understand Arab culture.

Egypt seemed a good place to start. Egypt is by far the most populous Arab state. And although Egypt is a poor country in per-capita-income terms, its economy is larger than Saudi Arabia's. Historically Egypt has been the most westward-looking of Arab countries. A Napoleonic invasion, an Albanian pasha named Muhammad Ali, and a British takeover gave Egyptians plenty to look at. The modern Islamist movement can be dated from the founding of the

Muslim Brotherhood by an Egyptian schoolteacher, Hassan al-Banna, in 1928. Two of Osama bin Laden's closest aides, Ayman al-Zawahiri and the late Muhammad Atef, came from Egypt, as did Mohammed Atta, who led the September 11 hijackings. And there is this thing called the "Arab street," which various serious people take seriously. In the November 11, 2001, *New York Times* John Kifner wrote, "It is on just this Arab . . . street that President Bush must fight in his war against Osama bin Laden." On January 24, 2002, Chris Matthews said on the television program *Hardball,* "America's been fighting another kind of war to win the hearts and minds of the Arab street." And on November 16, 2001, NBC *Nightly News* reporter Martin Fletcher, broadcasting from Cairo, declared, "The battleground isn't only in Afghanistan; it's here in the Arab street." Well, Cairo has thousands of miles of street.

But there's a problem with Egypt. It's been around for five millennia. America is only three human life spans in age. I'm an American born and bred, so were my folks, and . . . How could the same small part of America vote for both Rudolph Giuliani *and* Hillary Clinton? How could any parts of America elect action-figure toys as governors? Why haven't they been noticeably worse than other governors? Why is the fastest-growing spectator sport in America watching cars turn left? How come I've never heard of anyone— Linkin Park, Ludacris, OutKast—on the *Billboard* Top 50? Why can't they spell? By what means did the Amazon.com list of best-sellers in 2001 come to contain *The Widsom of Menopause, Self Matters, Look Great Naked,* and *BodyChange*— the last by someone called Montel Williams, who is on daytime TV? Have you ever *watched* daytime TV? Who are these people taking DNA tests to see which one molested the Rottweiler?

I don't understand anything about America's culture. What could I hope to learn about Egypt's? In fact, quite a bit—before I'd been officially in the country for more than a minute. Coming through passport control, I was detained by a solemn fellow who showed me a badge. In his well-ironed dress-down Friday clothing, clean grooming, and chilly politeness, he was the exact counterpart of a Mossad agent who had detained me at Ben-Gurion Airport eight months before. "I would like to ask you a few questions about why you are visiting Egypt," the solemn fellow said.

My tour operator, carrying a placard with my name completely misspelled, swooped in with a great bustle: "We are a prominent Egyptian tourism company! Government-licensed! This man is a valued client! Tourism is in a ruinous state! Do you even *see* another tourist?! What will become of Egypt's foreign-reserve situation?!"—although that was all body language. I believe the only thing my tour operator actually said to the intelligence officer was "He's with me." Away we went. Have your travel agent try that with the Mossad or the FBI.

There was another lesson in just the drive through Cairo from the airport, on the far east side of town, to my hotel, by the pyramids in the west. It's the lesson of all swollen capitals in societies with uncompetitive economies. "In a competitive society," the economist Friedrich Hayek once said, "most things can be had at a price—though it is often a cruelly high price we have to pay . . . The alternative is . . . the favor of the mighty." The mighty have their seat in the capital. Better stick close to their chair legs and napkins to get a crumb from the mighty's table.

Cairo is the largest city in the Middle East and Africa, with more than 16 million people, most of whom were offering to carry my luggage at the airport. And they were more persistent than the secret police. Annex Damascus to Beirut, Baghdad, Kuwait City, Jerusalem, and Riyadh (what a war you'd have!) and you still wouldn't get Cairo. Almost a quarter of the people in Egypt live in the city, a long haul from the sea, on the site of an old fort of middling strategic importance, distant from natural resources or any traditional means of creating wealth except the Nile farmlands now under Cairo pavement. Think of a capital of the United States located in a Maryland swamp with 70 million Americans gathered there to be close to Medicare benefits, Fannie Mae, and Small Business Administration loan originations.

After ninety minutes in my tour van I realized: so vast is Cairo, there really is no way across it. At least no way with my eyes open. The traffic is too scary. We Americans, who invented traffic, are always being startled by the forms into which it has evolved around the world. (God, if He's a Darwinian, may be similarly aghast at life.) But most foreign driving has the advantage of either brevity, in its breakneck pace, or safe-if-sorry periods of complete rest, in jam-ups. Cairenes achieve the prolonged bravado of NASCAR drivers while also turning any direction they want in congestion worse than L.A.'s during an O.J. freeway chase.

When I could bear to peek, I saw traffic cops—not in ones or twos but in committees, set up at intersections and acting with the efficiency and decisiveness usual to committees. And I saw a driving school. What could the instruction be like? "No, no, Anwar, *faster* through the stop sign, and make your left from the *far right* lane." Surely John Kifner,

Chris Matthews, and NBC News are kidding when they use "Arab street" as a metaphor for anything in the Middle East. Or, considering the history of the Middle East, maybe they aren't.

The bar at the Mena House Hotel, in Giza, has half a dozen floor-to-ceiling windows, and the view of the Great Pyramid of Khufu fills them all. A number of people were in the bar. Unfortunately for business, they all worked there. Several waiters craned their necks, trying to catch my eye. Across the roomful of empty tables a musical trio abandoned their classical repertoire and began cracking one another up with jazz noodlings of "Woman in Love." Out in the lobby, by the front door, was an unattended metal detector. Every now and then it emitted a merry buzz, and everyone in the bar looked up hopefully, only to see another idle taxi driver on his way to the men's room.

I wandered across the street to the pyramid complex, now closed for the evening. Behind a police station was a stable yard with horses and camels kept for foreign visitors who, in better times, when there *are* foreign visitors, want a Sheik of VisaCard moment on their home videos. There I met Mousa, who presented himself, in so many words, as the Night Mayor of Khufu. He promised a forbidden after-hours tour.

"Can we climb to the top?" I asked.

"It is forbidden."

We walked through an alley, past a large hole in the wall that surrounds the pyramid complex. "Japanese tourists did this," said Mousa, "to climb to the top." Has anyone had any success understanding Japanese culture?

Mousa worked as an unlicensed guide from eight at night until two-thirty in the morning. He supported, he said, his father, his wife, three daughters, his sister whose husband had died, and his sister's child. "I must tell my father there is one tourist in Egypt,". said Mousa.

I asked him about the September 11 terrorist attacks. "Whoever does this ruins my life," said Mousa. "I do not know who does this."

Perhaps taking my silence as a rebuke, Mousa continued, "Maybe Osama bin Laden does this." He warmed to his theme. "Osama bin Laden does the killing in Luxor." Mousa was referring to the murder of fifty-eight tourists at the Mortuary Temple of Queen Hatshepsut, in November 1997. And Mousa may have had a point. According to Egyptian police, one of the killers, Midhat Mohammed Abdel-Rahman, had traveled to Afghanistan and Sudan for terrorist training. "Osama lives in Egypt before," Mousa said. (Maybe not, but the family business, Binladen Brothers for Contracting and Industry, employs forty thousand Egyptians.) "And has no respect for Egypt. He tries to destroy our country."

We walked across the outskirts of the village of Nazlet as-Samaan. The people who helped with the building of the pyramids once lived here. Now the people who help with the gawking do. We went behind the Sphinx into the quarry where pyramid makings were cut, forty-six hundred years ago, and climbed to the edge of the Giza Plateau. There was Khufu—immense, 449 feet high, almost exactly 745 feet on each side.

The stones aren't as big as those the Hebrews in *The Ten Commandments* hauled across the movie screen. The real blocks of granite and limestone are about the size of industrial air-conditioning units on strip-mall roofs. They look depressingly unfake. You can imagine the awful labor of heaving and pulling these rocks—2.3 million of them, according to Mousa.

There is a question that less sophisticated Americans ask (and more sophisticated Americans would like to): Why are the people in the Middle East so crazy? Here, at the pyramids, was an answer from the earliest days of civilization: people have always been crazy.

A certain amount of craziness, if not possessed already, can be acquired trying to walk in Cairo. The city is well supplied with sidewalks, but they just take you around the block. You can't step off them because of the traffic. The locals manage to cross streets. I began thinking that Cairenes employ some chapter of the ancient Egyptian Book of the Dead, which I missed when I was a hippie, that tells them how to keep going after they've been squashed between two trucks.

It took me forty-five minutes to cross the Shari El Corniche to get to the Nile embankment—and then, rather than try it again, I hiked almost a mile to what I thought was a walkway overpass. It wasn't an overpass. It was a stairway for pedestrian access to one of Cairo's few stretches of expressway. I guess this was installed for those bored with ordinary Cairo jaywalking: a sort of double-black-diamond run for the Cairo shoe slalom. Later, in a taxi on this same expressway, my driver missed an exit and backed up to it from somewhere beyond the next one.

Cairo's buildings are Cairo's traffic in concrete. Every structure seems halfway through construction or halfway through demolition, and some seem to be undergoing both.

This is modern Cairo. You can find old stones in the town if you let your tour guide drag you to them. My tour guide, Peter, did his best to show me a first-century Roman fort, the ninth-century mosque of Ibn Tulun, and Saladin's twelfth-century citadel. But even the pyramids are as beside the point in Cairo as the Dutch wall is on Wall Street. Essentially all of Cairo is modern. The population was only 570,100 in 1897. The number of residents has more than tripled in the past twenty-five years. I saw a cement truck, barrel turning, load ready to pour, driving down a Cairo street at two o'clock in the morning.

The upthrustings and downtearings in central Cairo's business district look the way they do in every busy place. Or they would if you could see them behind the profusion of blimp-sized billboards that look the way they do in every busy place. As it turns out, the Nile is just a river in Egypt—not nearly as wide as the Hudson River at the George Washington Bridge. Cairo's rich have river views and live, as most rich do nowadays, in apartment houses of faceless effrontery. The only apparent difference from the apartments of the American rich with river views is that in the Cairo apartments every single room has a huge chandelier.

But the emblematic building of Cairo is the small tower block—five or six stories designed in a fashion so functional that the Bauhaus architects were lapdogs of ornamentalism by comparison. Slab floors are supported by reinforced-concrete posts and beams, like the skeletons of timber-frame colonial farmhouses—and, like colonial farmhouses, the tower blocks tend sometimes to the rhomboid. The spaces between the posts are filled with jumbles of approximately brick-shaped bricks and punctuated, apparently at random, with little windows and balconies. The outside edges of poured-concrete staircases poke through the masonry, their runs and risers making zigzag patterns. Dried oozes of mortar cling to the brickwork. Water pipes and electric wires are tacked onto the outside walls as if in halfhearted, rust-staining homage to the Pompidou Center.

In Europe these myriad domiciles would look like self-storage units for the urban proletariat. In Egypt, concrete mosques are crammed between the tenements and festooned with colored lights—as if for Christmas decoration, except no red, just the green of Islam. Commerce hums on the ground floors in shops and restaurants, one called Pizza Hat. Roofs are adorned with the festive dishware of satellite TV. The walls of the little balconies are plastered and painted blindingly cheerful shades of swimming-pool blue and lawn-chemical green.

"Plain exteriors," said Peter, "mean less taxes to the government. Interiors are very often elaborate." And peering into bright living rooms, I could see another emblematic Cairo item—the astonishingly ugly sofa. An ideal Egyptian davenport has two Fontainebleaus' (the one in France and the one in Miami) worth of carving and gilt and is upholstered in plush, petit point, plaid, and paisley as if Donald Trump and Madame Pompadour and Queen Victoria and the Doors had gotten together to start a decorating firm. Often there's a pair of matching chairs.

You see the astonishingly ugly sofa everywhere—in the homes of the well-off and the otherwise, in hotel lobbies, office reception areas, furniture-store windows (of course), and, most spectacularly, on Egyptian television sitcom sets. One actor sits down on it and makes an exasperated face while the other actors gesticulate comically. I couldn't understand what was going on in Egyptian sitcoms, but I could tell it was more charming than Montel Williams.

I got to watch a lot of Egyptian TV, owing to a miscalculation in my attempt at cultural understanding. I'd arrived in Egypt in early December, in the middle of Ramadan. Not that Ramadan itself is hard to understand. It's a kind of Lent or extended Yom Kippur, with fasting from sunrise to sunset. Nothing is supposed to pass the lips, not even a smoke or a sip of water. And Egyptians, at least in public, observe the rules. Clubs and discos are closed. Coffeehouses are empty. People in airport lounges are reading the Koran aloud. I was changing money when the call to midday prayer came from the PA system of the local mosque. The bank guard put his rifle aside, unrolled a rug, and performed his devotions. Fortunately, bank robbers were as pious and made no depredations. But Ramadan also has the aspect of a monthlong Thanksgiving dinner with the family. When the sun goes down, everyone rushes home for the *iftar* feast. Another big meal, *suhour,* is served before dawn. There's a bit of Christmas, too, with shopping for toys and clothes to be given to children during the three days of *Eid al-fitr,* when the fasting is over. Stores are open at all hours of the night, and folks are out in the streets at three and four in the morning, children in tow. I'd been in Egypt for a week before I realized I was a diurnal creature in a nocturnal biosystem.

During the hours of daylight, Egyptians are—considering that they're hungry, thirsty, and really want a cigarette— remarkably cheerful. That is, when they're awake. People sleep late. Arriving in Egypt during Ramadan is like arriving in an American small town on a holiday weekend about the time that the bowl games come on. Ramadan is, in fact, Egypt's peak television-viewing period. "Best TV Land is in Ramadan," I heard an announcer say as I surfed past what might have been an Arabic version of *Late Night with Conan O'Brien*. The celebrity guests were sitting on an astonishingly ugly sofa.

The effusive, jolly ugliness of furniture suits a city that should be depressing but isn't. And the city should be squalid, too. It's an impoverished metropolis with a population density three times New York's. But Cairo is clean—if you don't count a sky that ranges in color from cheap-motel bedsheet to frightening diaper.

There's little begging, although plenty of *Whereyoufrom Youbuypostcardokay?* if you look like a tourist, and I do. Nobody is living on the street. The homeless, Peter explained, have teamed up with the lifeless. The city's huge Eastern and Southern Cemeteries are filled with house-sized mausoleums used as houses. The Egyptian government, surrendering to the perennial Cairo housing shortage, has provided the cemeteries with a modicum of water and electricity—a humane version of American big cities' just giving up and getting Target to provide the homeless with snappy Michael Graves–designed trash bags to sleep under.

According to Peter, there are postmortem sublets in the so-called City of the Dead. The tenant of record's heirs charge rent to the viable occupants, who have to make themselves scarce on holidays and special occasions, when bereaved families come to picnic or even spend the night with the deceased. Peter said there have been squatters among the tombs since the fourteenth century. But the taste for elaborate mausoleums goes back further in Egypt—and so, maybe, do the squats. Perhaps disaffected experimental colossus carvers, young barley-beer addicts, and aspiring scribes with papyrus sheets full of edgy new hieroglyphics had crash pads in the Great Pyramid of Khufu.

Peter and I went ten miles south to Memphis, the capital of Egypt during most of pharaonic times. For three and a half millennia Memphis was the most important city in the country. Then, in the tenth century, the Fatimid general Jauhar al Rumi pillaged its stones to build Cairo. The dikes were neglected. And now Memphis is gone beneath the silt of the Nile.

But the former capital's necropolis, Saqqara, survives, marked by the Step Pyramid of Djoser. The Step Pyramid was completed about 2635 B.C. Peter said, "This was the world's first stone building."

I said, "In a country that's nothing but stone, with not a tree for miles, surely somebody . . ."

"The ancient Egyptians," Peter said, "built their houses out of mud and their tombs out of stone—to last for eternity." Most of Saqqara has collapsed into rubble.

Nearby is the Bent Pyramid. "This was the first pyramid of the true smooth-sided type," Peter said. To me it looked like a monument to middle-aged adultery—an affair begun with an aggressive angle of attack that couldn't be maintained. Apparently, building a pyramid was less straightforwardly Herculean than one might think. Peter explained, though not in these words, that there was more to it than making the top pointy so that the ancient Egyptians would know when to stop. Peter said the craft of pyramid building required a hundred years to perfect, leaving five pharaohs under large but irregular piles of stuff.

We went into the tomb of Mereruka, son-in-law of Pharaoh Teti, who reigned from 2355 to 2343 B.C. This tomb was a mastaba, a flat-roofed stone building, with thirty-three rooms. Peter claimed that only royals were allowed to depict the gods in their burial chambers, so Mereruka decorated his with scenes from daily life. And what a life. Carved onto the walls is a nice-looking family with plenty of household help. Frequent gourmet meals are served. There's surround-sound lute playing, many buff dancing girls, and goldsmiths coming up with something to placate the missus. Packs of happy naked kids—it must have been a progressive day-care center—play tug-of-war and Johnny-on-the-pony. Travel is as adventurous as anything in an Abercrombie & Kent brochure. Mereruka is shown spearing hippos (probably the bungee-jumping of his day). And one whole wall is devoted to a lively illustration of revenue enhancement. Serf personnel are—to put it in Enron terms—allowing their 401(k)s to be used to purchase the corporation's own stock (at the urging of supervisors with sticks).

Mereruka did well for himself while his wife's dad was running the show. I was looking at a recognizable yuppie paradise. Nothing here would have been strange to the Reagan merger-and-acquisition years or the dot-com boom. All it lacked was golf.

And yet I was also looking at thirty-three rooms of tomb, every one of which was to be filled with custom-made furniture, precious jewels, designer-label kilts and sandals, supermodel-endorsed eye kohl, vintage grand-cru palm-sap wine, and enough meals-to-go to last forever, not to mention archaeological treasures and priceless items of ancient Egyptian art. Plus there was that mummification, which probably cost more than a year at a spa.

Mereruka had invested the proceeds of his peak earning years in worm's meat. I was standing in his Aspen ski lodge, his Hamptons beach house, his Gulfstream jet, the professional sports team he never owned, the college education of his kids. (And in the end, Mereruka's tomb was never finished. Teti's successor, Pepy I, may have been one of those churlish brothers-in-law determined to get the deadwood out of the family business.)

There's a temptation to think that understating an ancient culture is easier, or at least less hectic, than understanding its contemporary offspring. The ancient culture holds still for inspection and doesn't produce new, confusing events such as a fresh episode of *Survivor* just after three thousand people were voted off the island of Manhattan.

But giant burial vaults can't have been an economically efficient investment of surplus capital. Riches could have been channeled into more productive use. Channeled literally, as in digging a canal across the flatland between the Nile Delta and the Gulf of Suez. But none was dug until after Darius, the Persian emperor, had conquered Egypt, in the sixth century B.C. Instead, when pharaohs wanted to trade along the Red Sea coast, they dismantled their boats, hauled them through the eastern desert, and put them back together. The Egyptians did not smelt iron. They didn't even discover bronze until the Middle Kingdom, a thousand years after the civilization was founded. Irrigation was accomplished with buckets on the ends of long levers or by carrying pots slung from yokes. The waterwheel wasn't introduced until the Persian invasion. And before the Persians there wasn't such a thing as money. The ancient Egyptian technological innovation of note (besides the enormous triangular four-sided sepulcher stack) was papyrus paper. According to the Egyptologist Cyril Aldred, the ready availability of paper "made the highly organized Egyptian state possible," for the privilege of living in which the Egyptian peasantry paid 50 percent of its produce in taxes.

Even so, I felt that I emerged from Mereruka's tomb into a poorer, more woebegone country. Of course, I didn't. Egypt today has a per capita gross domestic product of $3,600. The Organization for Economic Cooperation and Development estimates that before the Industrial Revolution, world per capita GDP was about $650 (in 1990 dollars). In 1820 Great Britain was the richest country on earth, with a per capita GDP of only $1,756. In wealth-per-person terms, merrie olde England was a Ghana. The ancient world seems rich to us because its DVDs of *Sex and the City* have survived rather than its kinescopes of *The Honeymooners*. And disparities in income, so shocking to our contemporary sensibilities, can't have been less. Consider the negative net worth of the slaves. They didn't have a title to, or even a mortgage on, themselves.

That said, in the fields and palm groves along the Nile are low mud houses of a kind unchanged since the days of Teti and Pepy. Identical homes are on display in miniature at the Egyptian Museum in Cairo—part of the LEGOLAND of peasantry and servitude that was placed as an offering in a pharaoh's crypt.

These Nile-side domiciles, in contrast to the City of the Dead, have been supplied with few electrical wires. Running water has in fact been taken away. Nile floods are now contained by the Aswan High Dam, and Egypt's fellaheen must use commercial fertilizer to do the job that muck did for eons.

So the farmers by the millions move to Cairo, and between the remaining baked-earth homesteads rise the weekend villas of plutocrat Cairenes. The villas would do credit to any gated community in Boca Raton. But the villas are the product of a path to success unfamiliar to Boca (if not to Mereruka). "Who can afford these places?" I asked Peter, who has a Ph.D. in Egyptology, as does his wife. They struggle to support two kids.

"Officials," he said. "And belly dancers."

Other paths to success are steeper. Peter took me to one of the numerous "carpet schools" along the Memphis-Giza road. Here children age ten and up were engaged in—pedagogical alibis and apprenticeship hooey aside—child labor. Also, some of the children looked more like eight than ten.

There was nothing Dickensian about the well-lit, swept, and airy ground floor full of looms. The manager said that the boys and girls were paid "to give them encouragement" and that "maybe they'll be able to get a job in the company's factory," although I had a feeling this *was* the factory. He assured me that his charges received academic instruction similar to that in the government schools. And maybe they do. Scribbled on one weaving frame was graffiti in English that read, "I will always be looling you." I watched little-kid fingers move with blurring speed among warp and woof and saw little-kid faces puckered in grim expertise. I'll never buy a handmade rug again.

Although I bought one. Small, expectant eyes were upon me. "September eleven is like a black day to us," the manager said. Is rug weaving really any worse than PlayStation 2? Maybe not; but since I got back from Egypt, wall-to-wall carpet made on automatic machines by unionized labor is looking better—the orange shag kind included.

To blame al Qaeda on poverty like Egypt's is, as I had told Rhona on the BBC, a slur on the poor. The September 11 attackers were taking flying lessons in America, not rug-weaving lessons in a village on the Nile. Yet there must be some economic, or political-economic, roots to the burning—flaming, bursting, exploding—bush of current events. Fouad Ajami, the author of *The Dream Palace of the Arabs* and professor at the Johns Hopkins School of Advanced International Studies, has written, "Atta struck at us because he could not take down Mr. Mubarak's world, because in the burdened, crowded land of the Egyptian dictator there is very little offered younger Egyptians save for the steady narcotic of anti-Americanism and anti-Zionism."

Narcotics aside, this "very little offered" raises a question about Arab culture. Why has Egypt—and the whole Arab world—made relatively little economic progress? Even the oil-flush Gulf states have not become rich the way we understand rich in the West. Kuwait is little more than an oil spigot with people sitting on top, and all they have to do is turn the tap. But Kuwait's per capita GDP is $15,000, while utterly resourceless Luxembourg's is $36,400.

Egypt of yore may have been economically sclerotic, but modern Egyptians can't really blame their ancient civilization.

At least they *had* a civilization, which is more than we did—
or, to judge by daytime television, do yet. And Islam didn't
destroy that civilization any more than the Persians, the
Ptolemites, the Romans, and the Byzantines had before. The
capitulation of Egypt to the Arabs was brokered by the Christian patriarch of Alexandria in 642, on condition of security
for persons and property and with religious freedom guar-
anteed in return for payment of tribute.

The Arab world began with a number of economic ad-
vantages besides tribute. It had a common language, a uni-
fied government, and territory that sat athwart the trade
from the Orient to the Mediterranean—Z's "strategic land
bridge." To move goods by any other route was to risk—
between the Mongols and the deep blue sea—getting very
wet or dead. The obligation of pilgrimage to Mecca stimu-
lated commerce and encouraged the general public to travel
the way nothing else would until the invention of frequent-
flyer miles and Disney World. A measure of law and order
existed, unlike in Europe, where there was none, and in
China, where there was too much. And Arabs had absorbed
the learning of Greco-Roman civilization centuries before
Europeans, in their Renaissance, began to pick scraps of it
out of the ruin they'd made of Greece and Rome. Also, the
Islamic religion has the right attitude. In the Koran, Sura
II, verse 275, states: "God hath permitted trade." The Koran
orders the use of honest weights and measures, the fulfill-
ment of contracts, and the payment of debts. And one of
the sayings attributed to Muhammad makes him not just
the Prophet of Allah but the prophet of Adam Smith: "Only
God can fix prices."

But something went wrong. How did the Arabs fall behind Europe, America, and now the Far East? It was prob-

ably nothing so air-filled as "The experimental model and European rational thought," or "the Protestant work ethic," or "Confucian values." Civilizations, like people, trip over smaller things. The answer may be as boring as a real estate title search (a title search, it may be noted, of real estate in the same neighborhood where the early Zionists were intent on buying).

Caliphs and sultans did not bestow feudal lands on a hereditary nobility. Fiefs were generally temporary. Land was given to a particular person for a certain time in return for military or other services. Agricultural estates were your salary. You got a raise by squeezing everything you could out of them. And you had to do it quickly, before you lost your job. There was no incentive to invest in the land, much less in the people who tilled it. This was a carnival concession. You were never going to see these rubes again.

The dearth of private land in the Islamic world is of a piece with the excessive government centralization that has always plagued the civilizations of the Fertile Crescent. Farming in much of the area requires irrigation, a horribly communal activity like being trapped in an endless Amish barn raising. Then the people of the region went and invented writing. Writing is the enabler of bureaucracy. Bureaucracy leads to government on the Department of Motor Vehicles model, with patronage jobs, wire pulling, and a political hack of a boss.

The Muslim conquerors of the Fertile Crescent may have come from independent and roughly democratic Arab tribes, but they quickly glommed on to state power, as did their Seljuk and Ottoman Turk successors. Despite the laissez-faire prescriptions of the Koran, and the Prophet's warnings against price controls, the Islamic state proceeded, like its predecessors, to interfere grossly with the economy. The preeminent Western historian of Islam, Bernard Lewis, estimates that Middle East agricultural yields began a decline in late Roman times that has continued almost to the present day. As for commerce, Lewis has written, "Governments seemed to have reasoned that if they could earn so much a year by taxing the pepper trade, they could earn even more by taking it over entirely." This works so well in Cuba. Lewis argues that Islamic commercial wealth was not destroyed by European innovations in ocean shipping. Rather, Europeans were driven to the sea lanes because, in the 1400s, the Mamluk sultan of Egypt nationalized the spice trade and forced the Kmart of nutmeg-and-ginger caravans into receivership.

The economic decline can be measured by the number of people the economy was able to support. The Egyptian historian Afaf Marsot believes that the population of Egypt at the time of the Arab conquest was 20 to 30 million. By the late 1700s it was about 3 million.

Mamluk sultan-ish behavior persisted into the modern era. Gamal Abdel Nasser ruled Egypt from 1952 to 1970, and his political slogan said everything that can be said about centralization: "We are all Nasser." He nationalized banks, insurance companies, and other major enterprises. Land ownership was limited to around forty acres, about the size of the plot on which the average fellaheen was starving. Imports were radically reduced, and a broad program of "import substitution" was effected. I'll have a McGoat and a large order of papyrus fries. Marsot says of the Nasser regime, "The real administration was carried out through exceptional decrees, through patron-client relationships, through appeals to individuals in power."

Sounds like Enron to me. But Alan Greenspan says America's economy is doing fine. And so, to some extent, is Egypt's. Reforms and privatizations were begun by Anwar Sadat and have continued under Hosni Mubarak. Egypt's GDP grew by an average of 5.05 percent a year from 1997 to 2000. I had dinner with some Egyptians in the steel business. Their business talk sounded like any business talk. When they discussed the downturn in structural steel demand resulting from global recession and the September 11 attacks, they may have meant "We are all Nasser," but what they said was "We are all broke." Though considering the size of the restaurant check they picked up, they didn't really mean it.

Shopkeepers, although glum about the current situation, did not seem to be in a mood of permanent despair. I spent a pleasant hour in the Khan al-Khalili bazaar lounging atop rolls of brilliantly striped Egyptian canvas talking to a maker of drawstring pokes and backpacks. He was interested to hear about the L.L.Bean boat bag and how there are people called WASPs in America who can't so much as send a kid and the nanny to the beach club without employing three or four of these stiff cotton sacks.

I had lunch with an Egyptian who had been born in the United States. When he was in high school, in suburban Chicago, he became serious about religion and observed Ramadan with rigor. Then he went to Egypt to work as a journalist, and now, in Ramadan, he was having lunch. "My sister is a Christian fundamentalist," I said. "She wouldn't crash a plane into the World Trade Center, but she might land pretty hard on somebody teaching evolution in school."

"A lot of people don't make that connection," the Egyptian journalist from Chicago said.

But the movement of Egypt's material culture into middle-class prosperity is not happening fast enough to simply turn them into us. (And since I began watching American daytime television, I'm not sure I want it to.) Also, a small item in the December 10, 2001, edition of *The Egyptian Gazette* indicates that the fatal bull's-eye of centralization remains pinned to the Egyptian economy. "Minister of Planning Othman Mohammed Othman," the item read, "said the government was unable to manage the economy alone." In addition, Egypt continues to suffer from the corruption that's bred when profit lies down with politics. Transparency International's 2001 Corruption Perceptions Index rates Egypt 3.6 on a scale of 10, with 10 being the least corrupt. Finland is 9.9. Drug-lord-beleaguered Colombia, at 3.8, is less corrupt than Egypt.

Five millennia of economic tomfoolery is bound to leave Egyptians confused about economic principles. On the subject of free trade, M. Ali Ibrahim, who writes the front-page "Tell Me More" column for *The Egyptian Gazette,* can sound like Pat Buchanan on a bad-chest-hair day. "Immediate restrictions must be introduced to drastically reduce imports," Ibrahim wrote on December 5, 2001. "We waste millions of dollars on provocative imported commodities, dog food, nuts and ice cream." Ibrahim cited the work of Mahmoud Bazaraa, "an economics expert" who claims "that a liberal economy doesn't mean opening wide the doors for imports." A few days later Ibrahim's column was titled: "Tell Me More . . . About imported prayer beads, how they're bankrupting local merchants."

* * *

"In the United States," I said to Peter, "we're worried about Egyptian Islamic extremism. So what's with all the crosses on the Cairo skyline?"

"I'm Christian," Peter said. The owners of his tour company were also Christians, as were most of its employees.

"How many Egyptians are Christian?" I asked.

"Many," said Peter, "but I don't know how many."

Most Egyptian Christians are members of the Coptic Church. Fouad Ajami writes, "The demographic weight of the Copts is one of the great riddles of Egypt." Ajami quotes the political historian Rifaat Said, who says, "We count everything in Egypt: cups, shoes, books. The only thing we don't count are the Copts." Copts make up 6 percent of the Egyptian population (the official estimate) or 10 percent (the historian Afaf Marsot's estimate) or 12 percent (the estimate from the American organization, Center for Religious Freedom, in Washington, D.C.). Only 11 percent of Swedes go to church. Egypt may be a more Christian country than Sweden.

Copts believe that the nature of Jesus Christ was completely divine. Other Christians believe that the nature of Jesus was both divine and human. This used to be something you could get killed over. And it still is. Muslims believe that the nature of Jesus was just plain human. Islamic-extremist violence has been aimed at fellow Egyptians as well as at foreign tourists. In January 2000, in the town of Al-Kosheh, anti-Copt rioting resulted in the deaths of twenty-two Christians.

But Afaf Marsot claims that the Copts were treated better by their Muslim conquerors than by their Byzantine overlords, who considered them heretics. Copts were incorporated into the Arab government. Bernard Lewis says that as late as the thirteenth and fourteenth centuries Muslims were complaining that Copts were running the administration. They're still there. Boutros Boutros-Ghali, a Copt, was Mubarak's deputy prime minister for foreign affairs before becoming secretary-general of the UN.

Peter took me to the Coptic quarter of Cairo. We saw a welter of Christian worship going on—although it was a weekday—and more than a few Santa decorations. Peter showed me where Pharaoh's daughter found Moses floating in a basket. The basement grotto *was* flooded, so this may have been the spot. No, I'm getting mixed up in my notes. The flooded grotto was the place where Jesus and Mary and Joseph—when Herod the Great was killing all those babies—sought shelter on their flight into Egypt. I hope they brought galoshes. The Church of Saint Sergius, one of the oldest Christian churches in Egypt, was constructed over the grotto in the fifth century. To support one end of a door lintel in the church, a Roman column was used with its capital flat on the floor—in case you think it's only Muslims who turn civilization upside down.

The place where Moses was found is in the Ben Ezra Synagogue, which is no longer used for daily worship. "Fewer than a hundred Jews are left in Egypt," Peter said. "All of them are over seventy. There are maybe twenty synagogues in Egypt. Only one is open."

When Ben Ezra was restored in the nineteenth century, thousands of manuscripts were discovered, dating back to the eleventh century. "It is the habit of the Jews all over the world," Peter said, "to write the story of their lives and hide these writings in certain places." I was thinking of Anne Frank, but I don't believe Peter was. He talked about "the closed society of the Jews" and said, "We do not forget the help the Jews gave the Hyksos." These were the pharaohs of the Fifteenth Dynasty, apparently of Semitic origin, who ruled Egypt after the fall of the Middle Kingdom, 3,650 years ago. Peter was still irked. "The Jews came to Egypt three times," he said, frowning, "with Joseph, with Ptolemy, and in 1492." (And with baby Jesus in A.D. 1.) By the way, the Jews were moderately well treated on each occasion—although there seems to have been a flare-up of ill feeling about the time of the Exodus. And now, of course.

In December 2001, the big hit from Egypt's pop singer of the moment, Shaaban Abdel-Rahim, was "Ana Bakrah Israel" ("I Hate Israel"). Abdel-Rahim claimed the cassette had sold 5 million copies. In a week's worth of *Egyptian Gazettes*, each edition only eight to twelve pages long, I counted fifty-eight articles involving Israel. The December 12, 2001, issue alone had five, three of them on the front page. One piece, on December 10, cited "rumors that Mossad agents have secretly hidden magnetic strips inside Cleopatra cigarettes." The story noted that "strong electromagnetic fields are a health risk" and went on to mention "'lethal' magnetic belt buckles, seen as an Israeli plot to make Egyptians sterile."

The Egyptian Gazette, which the *Lonely Planet* guide calls "Egypt's awful daily English-language newspaper," is an anodyne (and anti-Osama) publication that turns up outside hotel room doors in the morning and is clearly meant to be read by foreigners, some of whom are likely to be Jewish. Much worse things are available from the Arab-language press, as is pointed out by the Middle East Media Research Institute, MEMRI, a pro-Israel organization that collects much worse things from the Arabic-language press.

According to MEMRI the following items appeared in the Egyptian government dailies *Al-Akhbar* and *Al-Ahram* from April to August 2001:

Mahmoud Muhammad Khadhr, a cleric from Cairo's Al-Azhar University, posed the rhetorical question "Did Hitler attack the Jews or did their crime deserve even more? . . . The Zionists were a fifth column in Germany, and they betrayed the country that hosted them."

Dr. Mahmoud Al-Said Al-Kurdi stated, "The Talmud, the second holiest book for the Jews, determines that the 'matzahs' of Atonement Day must be kneaded 'with blood' from a non-Jew. The preference is for the blood of youths after raping them!"

And journalist Fahmi Huweidi described his feelings after a suicide bombing: "I cannot hide my happiness about the martyrdom operation that took place in Jerusalem last Thursday. I won't deny that it liberated me from the sorrow and misery that have overtaken me over the past weeks."

Fouad Ajami's "narcotic of anti-Zionism" packs a punch.

And maybe so does poetic license. I mentioned that al Qaeda may have a Yeats. It may have worse than that. In *The Dream Palace of the Arabs*, Ajami explains that Arab society puts a great value on poetic expression—a 1950s-Smith-College-girl-with-her-head-in-the-oven value. In the March 10, 2002, *New York Times Book Review*, Judith Shulevitz wrote about Osama bin Laden's recitation of poetry on one of his videotapes (a poem plagiarized from Jordanian poet Yusuf Abu Hilalah). Shulevitz said that this recitation "would burnish bin Laden's reputation in a way that Americans might not readily understand, given the high premium placed in the Middle East on poetic eloquence, even in a political leader." And it is hard to imagine George W. Bush cribbing from Sylvia Plath in his post–September 11 address to the joint session of Congress:

> *Out of the ash*
> *I rise with my red hair*
> *And I eat men like air.*

Ajami quotes the poet Nizar Qabbani, who said that the Arab is the "quintessential poetic being" and that poetry is "written on the forehead of every Arab." Anyone who has had a similar experience of letting his words get ahead of his frontal lobes knows where this can lead. Maybe, in the calumnies of *Al-Akhbar,* there is a kinship to Plath's poem "Daddy," in which she addressed her father: "Panzer-man, panzer-man, O You—" Otto Plath was a Boston University professor of biology and an expert on bees.

Or maybe what we're hearing in *Al-Akhbar* is prosaic hate. But either way, the reality was that it had been almost thirty years since the last war between Egypt and Israel. Americans in my parents' generation were pretty mad at the Japs. They got over it. And by the 1970s they were driving Datsuns.

I flew to Luxor. Trying to understand a culture by being a tourist is famously useless. But trying to understand Egypt without being a tourist would be worse than useless. Egypt is the cradle of tourism. Herodotus was a tourist here in the fifth century B.C. And the First Dynasty of the pharaohs was as far removed in time from Herodotus as he is from us. Tourism was the source of history's original failure of cultural understanding. Cyril Aldred writes that ancient Greek and Roman vacationers in Egypt "never really understood Egyptian religion and were inclined to see in inexplicable acts and beliefs a more profound significance than actually existed." Thus the concept of the "inscrutable Orient," the idea of the "mysterious East."

Luxor is the site of the ancient sacred city of Thebes, 419 miles upstream from Cairo. The Temple of Luxor is downtown, and nearby are the Colossi of Memnon, Karnak Temple, Hatshepsut's Temple, the Valley of the Kings, the Valley of the Queens, and the Ramesseum, with the gigantic shattered statue of Rameses II that inspired Shelley to write "Ozymandias."

> *And on the pedestal these words appear:*
> *"My name is Ozymandias, king of kings:*
> *Look on my works, ye Mighty, and*
>   *despair!"*
> *Nothing beside remains. Round the decay*
> *Of that colossal wreck other than ticket*
>   *booths, soda-pop stands,*
>   *souvenir stalls, dozing guards, and*
>   *200 men in galabias asking,*
>   *"WhereyoufromYoubuypostcardokay?"*

At the Sheraton Hotel in Luxor a few tourists were braving the geopolitics—some Europeans, a couple of Japanese, and a scattering of doughty American retirees of the type who can't get along without L.L.Bean boat bags. I heard a voice in the Sheraton bar saying, with a plummy English accent, "The reason *I* got fired . . ."

My guide in Luxor, Ibrahim, was one of those people— rare among tour guides—who are impelled to tell the truth. His description of the mummification process was sickening.

I asked Ibrahim about the war on terror. "Egyptians support America's actions in Afghanistan," he said, and paused. "Most do. But I must tell you the truth, others do not. Maybe thirty percent do. I am Christian. All Christians support America's actions." He paused again. "But maybe ninety percent of Egyptians are opposed."

Luxor's tombs and temples were interesting—briefly. Ibrahim *would* recount the attributes, the ancestry, and the avatars of every mythological figure portrayed. He came to a brief, embarrassed halt only at Min, who is represented with a healthy erection. And so Min might well be represented, given the lissome and un-burka'd female deities on the tomb and temple walls. The ancient Egyptian pantheon seems to have read the Amazon.com best-seller *Look Great Naked* in an earlier edition.

But the mild thrill of anachronistic eroticism wears off, the gimmick of puppy-headed gods palls, and a satiety with ritual mumbo jumbo sets in. Too much Egyptian art in a day produces moods that go rapidly from Hobbit-jaded to child-wizard-bored to the feeling of being in a vegetarian restaurant with a blind date who's talking feng shui. Ibrahim took me to just such a restaurant near the Valley of the Kings, although it became vegetarian, for me, only after Ibrahim suggested I look in the kitchen.

From the restaurant's terrace I could also look up and down the Nile. The land of Egypt is nearly seven hundred miles long and, for most of that distance, effectively about seven miles wide. How did this affect a culture? Did people try to make their lives long and narrow? The funerary monuments around Luxor are a huge pharaonic Keogh plan meant to fund an eternal hereafter just like the therebefore.

I could be wrong. What will be left of our civilization five thousand years hence? Probably the ruins of our interstate highway system. The tourists of some future age will wonder, as I wondered at the Valley of the Kings, "Why were these people so obsessed with where they were going instead of where they were?"

But our rest stops won't present the same opportunities for looting. ("A New Jersey Devils snow globe!") All the ancient Egyptian tombs were robbed, many by contemporaries of the deceased. Even the famed trove of Tutankhamen was picked over not long after it was sealed. Suspicions arise of an inside job. A pharaoh's kids had motive, means, and opportunity. They'd been bilked of their inheritance, knew where the tomb was, and were paying the salaries of the guards.

"Didn't Grandpa have a set of solid-gold dinner plates just like this?"

"Finish your papyrus fries."

Nowadays the tombs are well protected. And so are their visitors. After the 1997 terrorist attack at Hatshepsut's Temple, the corps of black-clad elite Tourist Police was expanded and given special training. I saw one of them sitting in a squad car with a Furby hanging from the rearview mirror.

The Tourist Police were present in force at the Karnak temple complex. Karnak covers almost as much ground as Disneyland. The Great Hypostyle Hall alone has space enough for a heck of an Ancient Egyptian Adventure ride—whizzing among the 134 gigantic stone pillars. Indeed, visitors once came to Karnak with a more Disney-fied attitude. In tintypes of nineteenth-century tourists, we see that there's room for a hundred men to stand on the capital of one of these columns. This was the kind of culturally insensitive thing tourists used to do. Now they're herded into sound-and-light shows.

The Karnak *son et lumière* began with Wagnerian music and male and female recorded voices bouncing back and forth between widely separated speakers in the manner of sound-effects records from the early days of stereo. I forget what the female voice was pretending to be. The male voice was Amon-Ra—a Middle Kingdom syncretism of Ra, the sun deity, and a local goose god, the Great Cackler, who laid the cosmic egg.

The language of the performance was as poetic as anything that bin Laden was snapping his fingers to in the coffeehouses of the Shah-i-Kot Valley. "I am Amon-Ra," said the male voice. "The waters of the Nile sprout from my sandals." The *lumière* part consisted mostly of plunging us into darkness while we hung around in the supposedly spiritual ruins. Some of the tourists took flash photos of the opacity. "Yes, definitely spirits," I heard one woman tourist say.

A Ramadan service was being broadcast over the loudspeaker of a mosque outside the Karnak walls. The *son et lumière* producers turned up their volume. The Muslim clerics turned up theirs. The producers responded in kind. So did the clerics.

If the pious Muslims had had Ibrahim translating the *son et lumière* into Arabic, there might have been more than a war of words. "I am the father of fathers, mother of mothers," announced Amon-Ra very loudly indeed. ". . . the salvation of Amon, the salvation of Ra, also the salvation of the crocodile, offered equally to all the compass points of earth and to you, new pilgrim to Thebes."

I was reminded of nothing so much as my dad in a fez, headed out for a night with the boys. Dad was a Thirty-second Degree Freemason and a member of the Ancient Egyptian Arabic Order of Nobles of the Mystic Shrine. It's hard to imagine a worse case of cultural misunderstanding than the cultures of Egypt and Arabia represented by Dad on a midget motorcycle in the Fourth of July parade. Or maybe Dad knew more than I thought. During the late nineteenth century Egypt's King Tawfiq was a member of a Masonic lodge, as were many of Egypt's reform-minded liberal elite.

The next night I visited the Temple of Luxor, mercifully in silence. Luxor was consecrated to the "Thebean Triad": Amon-Ra; his earth-mother consort, Mut; and their moon-god kid, Khonsu. The temple was constructed about 1300 B.C. and restored by Alexander the Great, who built a new sanctuary for Amon-Ra. "In the wrong place," said Ibrahim. "Properly it should be in the last room of the temple, not here in the antechamber." Alexander's sanctuary stands just inside the antechamber's original walls. One set of hieroglyphs and reliefs was carved a thousand years later than the other.

"You see the difference," said Ibrahim.

I didn't. There is a supposed dynamism to ancient Egyptian art. According to Cyril Aldred, "It is often possible for the expert to date a specimen to within a few years by its stylistic features alone." So the expert says. But the ancient Egyptian language, Aldred himself points out, "has no genuine active tense." He notes that the ancient Egyptians did not adjust their calendar with the addition of an extra day every four years. They just let it slide for a millennium and a half until it got back into phase. When it came to art, I think the ancient Egyptians had a look going and decided to hang with it for three thousand years.

"Notice how the quality of decoration degenerated," Ibrahim said. An important part of cultural understanding is to understand that not all cultures progress.

Ibrahim and I went across the street and had dinner at McDonald's, where the quality of decoration had degenerated much further.

6

NOBEL SENTIMENTS

To mark the December 2001 hundredth anniversary of the Nobel Prize, Francis Crick, Nadine Gordimer, and José Saramago "in consultation with an extensive group of Nobel prize winners"—as the press release put it—issued a call to *do* something. The statement was signed by 103 Nobel laureates. It is printed in full below, with parenthetical exegesis by someone too dumb to ever get a Nobel, or even a MacArthur genius grant.

> The most profound danger to world peace in the coming years will stem not from the irrational acts of states or individuals but from the legitimate demands of the world's dispossessed.

(According to Nobel statement coordinator John C. Polanyi [Chemistry Prize 1986], the laureates' pronouncement was written before September 11. Don't rely on tips from Nobel laureates to win the Super Bowl office pool. And "irrational" is an interesting word choice. Aren't Nobel Prize winners supposed to understand how rationalization works? Maybe they mean "bad.")

Of these poor and disenfranchised . . .

(Why do political *bien-pensants* roll "dispossessed," "poor," and "disenfranchised" together, as if they have a natural correlation—like "ice," "cold," and "beer"? The Dalai Lama [Peace Prize 1989] is dispossessed. Your parish priest is poor. And Alan Greenspan, as a resident of the District of Columbia, is ineligible to vote in congressional elections.)

. . . the majority live a marginal existence in equatorial climates. Global warming, not of their making but originating with the wealthy few, will affect their fragile ecologies most.

(Did you see global warming coming out of left field? Anyway, blaming the onset of earth-is-toast on "the wealthy few" seems a tad unscientific for a document that is signed by sixty-five recipients of Nobels in chemistry and physics. The earth had temperature cycles when the wealthy few were lucky trilobites with extra-rich muck to delve in. And how are we going to solve the problems of those who "live a marginal existence in equatorial climates" such as that of Washington, D.C., if we don't produce more of the industrial prosperity that boils their weather? It's going to take a bunch of Nobel laureates to figure that out. Or not.)

Their situation will be desperate and manifestly unjust.

(Nice verb tense. In Congo, Haiti, Cambodia, and Liberia their situation right now is . . . ?)

> It cannot be expected, therefore, that in all cases they will be content to await the beneficence of the rich.

(I won't make a wisecrack about "cannot be expected . . . to await the beneficence of the rich." Specifically, I won't make the wisecrack "and should go get a job." This would be "manifestly unjust" to the hardworking poor—and dispossessed and disenfranchised—people of the world. Besides, if they got a job, it would worsen global warming.)

> If, then, we permit the devastating power of modern weaponry to spread through this combustible human landscape, we invite a conflagration that can engulf both rich and poor.

(Oh, I don't know. We did that in Afghanistan, and it was mostly the Taliban that got conflagrated.)

> The only hope for the future lies in cooperative international action . . .

(Obviously, when it came time for war with Iraq, the cooperative international action-takers at the UN weren't listening to Nobel laureates.)

> . . . legitimized by democracy.

(Well, *we're* a democracy—except occasionally in Florida, during electoral college vote counts.)

> It's time to turn our backs on the unilateral search for security, in which we seek to shelter behind walls.

117

(Good point. Walls collapse. On the other hand, concrete barriers that keep car bombs from being parked too close to public buildings are useful. So is baggage screening, and maybe a missile shield.)

> Instead we must persist in the quest for united action to counter global warming and a weaponised world.

("Weaponise" is my favorite new verb. The pen is mightier than the sword—until you weaponise your ballpoint to fight a man with a scimitar.)

> These twin goals will constitute vital components of stability as we move towards the wider degree of social justice that alone gives hope of peace.

(I thought "cooperative international action legitimized by democracy" was "the only hope." But I guess Nobel laureates, like anybody else, are entitled to change their minds. So "social justice" it is. However, you'd expect Nobel laureates to do the math on this. Divide the gross domestic product of the world by the world's population, and everyone gets $7,200 a year. What kind of basketball are we going to have if Shaquille O'Neal has to take a $21,422,800 pay cut? And a family of four in Tanzania making $28,000 *will* buy a used Toyota, which brings us back to global warming.)

> Some of the needed legal instruments are already at hand, such as the Anti-Ballistic Missile Treaty, the Convention on Climate Change, the Strategic Arms Reduction treaties, and the Comprehensive Test Ban Treaty.

(And don't forget the Kellogg-Briand Pact, the League of Nations Charter, and the Oslo accords.)

As concerned citizens . . .

(The rest of us aren't worried at all.)

. . . we urge all governments to commit to these goals that constitute steps on the way to the replacement of war by law.

(As in the Jim Crow laws, Hitler's Nuremberg Laws, South Africa's apartheid code, whatever legal gimcrackery Stalin used to prop up his show trials, etc.)

To survive in the world we have transformed, we must learn to think in a new way.

(They said it. I didn't.)

As never before, the future of each depends on the good of all.

(No—other way around. The future of all depends upon the self-interested good of each. Adam Smith did a lot of work in *The Wealth of Nations* showing this to be the case. See Book 1, Chapter 2: "It is not from the benevolence of the butcher, the brewer, or the baker, that we expect our dinner, but from their regard to their own interest." Although Adam Smith may be a little right-of-center to win a Nobel. Also, he's dead.)

To sum up, here we have a statement beginning with a thesis that had been disproved before it was uttered and ending with a palpable untruth. The logic meanders. The ideas are banal. The text exhibits a remarkable prolixity, considering that it's only 284 words long. Is this the best that 103 Nobel Prize winners can do?

Of course, it's always tempting to make fun of the Nobels. (Sidelight: Alfred Nobel owed his wealth not only to the invention of dynamite [see "combustible human landscape," above] but also to investment in his brothers' successful exploration for oil in Azerbaijan [see "combustible human landscape," above].) Making fun is especially tempting to those of us who will receive invitations to Stockholm only in the form of Scandinavian cruise-ship brochures. Let me give in to the temptation.

Ernest Hemingway but not James Joyce? Toni Morrison but not John Updike? Dario Fo? Selma Ottilia Lovisa Lagerlöf? (She wrote *The Wonderful Adventures of Nils,* a fanciful account of a young boy's travels across Sweden on the back of a goose.) And allow me to be the millionth person to point out that among the Nobel Peace Prize winners are Yasir Arafat, Shimon Peres, Henry Kissinger, Le Duc Tho, and International Physicians for the Prevention of Nuclear War ("If the mushroom cloud doesn't clear up, call me in the morning"). For all I know, the lists of prizewinners in physics, chemistry, medicine, and economics are just as wack. I'm not competent to judge. Although Cambridge University professor Brian Josephson (Physics Prize 1973) says, "There is a lot of evidence to support the existence of telepathy." And the codiscoverer of DNA, James Watson (Medicine Prize 1962), was, at age seventy-three, researching the effects of sunshine on sex drive.

Yet let us be generous. Prize-giving of any kind is no cinch. Nobel committee screwups notwithstanding, Nobel

Prize winners are smarter than we are. And Nobel Prize winners are doubtless as morally alert as we are. Even the Peace Prize winners are probably, on average, decent people. I scanned the list of hundredth-anniversary-statement signatories and didn't notice anyone in obvious need of a swift kick—the possible exception being statement coauthor José Saramago (Literature Prize 1998), a Portuguese Communist who wrote a novel, *The Gospel According to Jesus Christ,* in which Jesus tries to get out of being crucified and sleeps with Mary Magdalene. Henry Kissinger and Yasir Arafat did not apply their John Hancocks.

One hundred and three Nobel laureates have provided us with counsel on the political and social future of the world. Any such advice must be worth listening to, and I guess that includes the advice they've given us this time. But where are the words that stir men's souls? That turn their hearts? That change their minds? Where is the "We hold these truths to be self-evident . . ."? Where is even the "From each according to his ability, to each according to his needs"? For that matter, where is the "Where's the beef?"

Perhaps the Nobel laureates' statement should be understood as an indictment of our age. We could be living in an era so stupid that even the most intelligent among us are cement-heads. Possibly the laureates' statement is a simple proof, if proof were needed, that nothing good ever comes out of a committee. But maybe the statement contains a deeper message. Maybe the Nobel laureates are speaking, more powerfully than they realize, for radical democratization and perfect egalitarianism. Nothing in their statement indicates that the opinions of common men are worse or more foolish than the opinions of Nobel Prize winners. Let us have our international actions truly "legitimized by democracy." When it comes to questions of "What is to be done?" (to quote Lenin, as José Saramago might do), let's ask any old person. Let's ask Mom. Mom says, "Global warming or no global warming, it's cold out. Wear a hat."

7

WASHINGTON, D.C., DEMONSTRATIONS

April 2002

"I'll keep the mohawk until we stop killing people abroad."

—musician Eddie Vedder, quoted about
his hair in the April 11, 2002, issue
of *Rolling Stone*

The Palestinian Solidarity March had almost all the elements of a classic modern American political demonstration. On April 20, in downtown Washington, a constituency previously not heard from (or not listened to) turned out in impressive numbers. Its representatives looked respectable. They conducted themselves with dignity. They had a grievance. The only thing missing was an intelligible demand.

At least the Nobel laureates had silly ideas; the Palestinian Solidarity marchers wanted the people of the United States to . . . what? Abandon one of our few allies and take up the cause of Arab regimes that hate us? (And when an Arab regime, such as Saudi Arabia's, does profess friendship, it is the Eddie Haskell to our Wally Cleaver.) Should we, as more than a few placards suggested, GET OUT OF THE MIDDLE EAST? Then the frontline Arab states could have a free hand with Israel and recapture the glories of 1949, 1956, 1967, 1973, and 1982. Are we supposed to invade the region and sort things out? We did in 1991 and were soon to do it again. Support a Palestinian state? We've done that. Maybe we'd better continue to apply combinations of diplomatic pressure and aid incentives, keep formulating Oslo plans that settle everything (in Oslo), and go on folding and refolding that darned Road Map to Peace until it finally fits into the glove compartment of amity. Yet no one mounts a demonstration supporting current policies: the Million Muddlers-through March, with the masses chanting, "Five, four, three, two / We don't have a doggone clue!"

Israel stubbornly insists on existing. The foolish, despotic, and corrupt governments of the Arab countries stubbornly insist on various alternatives. The political and economic situation in Arab lands is so bad that it seems as if the only sensible thing for an Arab to do is get out and go someplace with freedom and opportunities. The people in the Palestinian Solidarity March had done so. Now they'd become a successful immigrant group exercising political power—exercising it to denounce American Zionists, a successful immigrant group exercising political power.

We are in the postmodern era of American political demonstrations. The Palestinian Solidarity March, an indignant crowd opposed, in a way, to itself, was marching around with little hope of achieving an objective—assuming there was one. This struck a chord. Thousands of other protesters joined in. They held a neo-demo, parodying the actions of the suffragettes, Cox's Army, the civil rights movement, and the Vietnam War protests. Seeking a clear political response has been replaced by consulting a Magic 8-ball of activist demands: "Reply Hazy, Demonstrate Again Later."

There were, in fact, three additional pointless marches in Washington on April 20. The Colombia Mobilization Festival of Hope and Resistance gathered at the Washington Monument. The U.S. drug-eradication policy was opposed. Millions of Americans have opposed that policy more effectively with mirrors, razor blades, and rolled-up dollar bills. The Colombia Mobilization also wanted the U.S. Army School of the Americas eliminated, although it has been and is now the Western Hemisphere Institute for Security Cooperation. This can no longer be called a training ground for Latin American dictators, because Castro is almost the only dictator left. And to judge by the number of Che T-shirts in the crowd, the Colombia Mobilization is on Castro's side.

Then there was the Mobilization for Global Justice, gathered in front of World Bank headquarters. This mobilization was claiming that World Bank development policies were all wrong. A little late. One of the World Bank's own economists, William Easterly, had already published a book in 2001, *The Elusive Quest for Growth,* claiming that World Bank development policies were all wrong.

And on the Ellipse, behind the White House, the U.S. war on terrorism and Israel's West Bank incursions were being denounced by ANSWER. Act Now to Stop War and End Racism is a group that awes any fan of acronyms. I was distracted from covering their event by an urge to scribble in my reporter's notebook, trying for a one-up: Quotidian Undergraduates Eagerly Supporting Terrorist Internment on Neptune.

The Palestinian Solidarity March began on Connecticut Avenue, at the Washington Hilton, where the somewhat acronym-impaired AIPAC, the American Israel Public Affairs Committee, was holding a conference. Many of the Arab-Americans arrived in family groups. Mothers and daughters were modestly garbed. Men wore crisp sport shirts and creased trousers. The other protesters, not all of them young, came dressed as young protesters. Covering of hair mingled with exposing of midriff. I didn't see anyone doing both, but a number of non-Arab marchers had kaffiyehs inexpertly plopped on their heads. A middle-aged man who was obviously not a Pakistani sported a *shalwar kameez* and walked down Connecticut eating from a box of Wheatette crackers.

According to the Sunday, April 21, *Washington Post,* "Organizers at the march privately urged participants to strike swastikas from their posters." They didn't comply. But many of the protest signs had the swastikas turned backward, perhaps in an effort to soften the Nazi reference: 卐 = SHARON = 卐. Thus some placards could be construed to mean "American Indian decorative motif = Prime Minister of Israel = Hindu good luck charm." Jews were among the marchers. JEWS FOR PEACE, read one sign. JEWS SAY NO TO ISRAELI STATE TERROR, read another. A chant went up nearby: "Two, four, six, eight / Israel is a racist state." Diverse advocacies mixed in the crowd: THE RICH MUST SHARE; DOWN WITH CORPORATE CAPITALISM; DESTROY ALL BORDERS; and a giant cardboard turtle labeled MOBILIZE. Everyone got along fine. A young man carried a crude birch-bark mock-up of a television captioned, "How much of your life is lived through a screen?" Another young man, a representative of something called the Independent Media Center, pedaled through the march on a bicycle equipped with a homemade duct-tape-and-PVC-pipe rig that held a video camera. Messages ranged from the disprovable (WE ARE ALL PALESTINIANS) to the dumbfoundingly true (TREES ARE NOT TERRORISTS—although the day before, in Washington, a tree had blown over in a thunderstorm and killed a passenger in a van.)

Some messages conveyed no sense: GIVE ME FREEDOM OR GIVE ME PALESTINE. Some conveyed too much: PRO PALESTINIAN AND PRO ISRAELI HUMAN RIGHTS IN THE OCCUPIED TERRITORIES. Some messages were open to interpretation. A young woman carried a picture of herself smiling broadly and embracing a large, happy mutt. Written beneath was "My dog has more rights than Palestinians."

Relations between the police and protesters were cordial. When the march reached the Connecticut Avenue tunnel under Dupont Circle, some of the marchers balked at entering, not without reason. The ventilation shafts rising from the underpass into the park were unguarded stink-bomb invitations. Washington police chief Charles Ramsey stepped in and led the way through.

The Solidarity March went down Eighteenth Street to the World Bank headquarters, where it was greeted with cheers and shouts of "Free, free Palestine!" There was pogo dancing at the Global Justice rally, and bare feet, and dissonant beating of drums, pots, and empty five-gallon plastic buckets. The effect was *Riverdance* if Ireland had been conquered by the deaf instead of the English. A baby carriage without a baby was pushed around with bongos and tambourines bungee-corded onto it and a sign reading RHYTHM WORKERS UNION. A couple was parading on stilts carrying GROW posters. The man's beard was braided. An American flag was burned, and so was a flag with yellow, blue, and red stripes. I asked what flag it was. No one seemed to know. "Colombia?" said someone. Two women in their twenties, festooned with buttons and stickers for various causes, ran toward the demonstrations holding hands and uttering squeals of gleeful anticipation.

I wasn't getting much information from the demonstrators. I have reached the stage in life when there's nothing I can do to keep from looking like a fifty-some-year-old man who should mind his own business. I had brought along Max Pappas, who does research work for me. Max, at twenty-six and with a couple of days' worth of stubble, can pass for an activist of some kind. Although, personally, I thought the cloth cap and olive-drab short-sleeved sport shirt that Max had selected, to blend in, made him look like a sports-car enthusiast on the way to bowling league. Max spotted a pack of bouncy coeds in yellow MOVEMENT T-shirts and immediately went to interview them. They were from Colby College, and the purpose of their organization was to go to lots of demonstrations. "If anyone has an idea," said one of the coeds, "you just come to the group and everyone will support you."

Other collegians had an even more supportive environment. An item in the Sunday *Washington Post* noted:

Students from the University of Wisconsin-Milwaukee and Milwaukee Area Technical College said their schools paid most of their expenses because they belong to a campus group, Students Peace Action Network. The schools provided vans for the trip and paid for hotels.

While Max was talking to the Colby coeds, a young woman with a tape recorder thrust a microphone in my face. She had a black hankie tied across her nose. I suppose she didn't mean this as a parody of a Muslim woman's veil. "Why are you at this protest?" she said, in a necessarily muffled voice.

"I'm a reporter," I said. She backed away.

Max talked to a man who was carrying a placard showing rainbow stripes, a peace sign, and a suggestion to "Envision a World." He was walking a tiny Pomeranian that did or did not have more rights than Palestinians. "Yeah, man," said the man, who appeared to be over forty, "when I get older, I want to join Greenpeace."

A fifteen-foot-wide balloon had been erected by the Rainforest Action Network. The balloon was decorated like a globe with a FOR SALE banner across it, but it was shaped like a small-town water tower or, maybe, a mushroom cloud. On one side of the balloon someone was speaking to not many people in Spanish while a young priest with blond streaks in his hair and wearing a fashion-forward sport coat got ready to take the mike. On the other side of the balloon was a protest against Citibank, whose Washington office is catty-corner to the World Bank. A speaker asked Citibank to "finance solar mortgages." The small group of listeners chanted—though not, I gathered, as a response to the speaker's request—"Hey, Citi, not with my money."

Max found campus feminists to interview. One admitted that the Taliban's treatment of women was terrible and said the United States should have done something earlier, "in the name of women."

"Wouldn't that involve war?" Max asked.

"Yeah, it's a tricky one," the feminist said. "There might be some nonviolent approach such as micro-lending."

A man stood inside an enormous, ill-made papier-mâché head of George Bush. The head did not bear a label. A bad portrait of George W. seemed to be the point. Other points being made in front of the World Bank: MORE WORLD/LESS BANK; PEACE THROUGH PEACEFUL MEANS; FUCK YOU CIA; NO MORE BHOPALS; REFUSE WAR/CHALLENGE DEMOCRACY; WE ARE ALL PALESTINIANS (on cartoons of Tibetan monks being beaten by Chinese soldiers and Vietnamese peasants being beaten by GIs); KEEP INDIA SECULAR; WE ARE COMPLICIT; and STOP THE COMMODIFICATION OF WATER (in a crowd where almost everyone was carrying a brand-name bottle of same). There was also a placard announcing that the carrier was a representative of an organization, "Suffering for African People," which critiqued the IMF's "structural adjustment programs." Both protester and protestee are in dire need of acronym consultation.

The Mobilization for Global Justice smelled of cats and patchouli oil and body odor. It joined with the Palestinian Solidarity March, and everyone moved in ragtag formation along H Street and down Thirteenth to Freedom Plaza, on the far side of the White House.

Counterdemonstrators were few. A Dockers-dressed mom and dad stood on H Street with their ten-year-old son. They held signs: GO BUSH and U.S. ♥ IT OR LEAVE IT. A few college-age protestors came out of the march to argue, though not with the parents, just with their child.

Some of the marchers—though none of the Arab-Americans—affected threatening attitudes. Their faces were masked. Their body language was angry. They shouted. But they didn't do anything. Several hirsute and not very clean young people wore bicycle helmets and MEDIC armbands. They hopped around nervously, giving, perhaps, a preview of some future socialized medicine. A kid waved an American flag that had corporate logos instead of stars on the blue field. He was wearing Adidas shoes, a Swiss Army watch, and a Mountain-smith backpack. Four of the Palestinian Solidarity marchers carried a makeshift litter bearing a girl wrapped in bandages and pretending to be injured or dead. The day was growing muggy, and the girl's companions sprinkled Evian on her face. A tourist bus got caught up in the march at Thirteenth and New York Avenue. Someone bobbed around in the crowd wearing an enormous gold-fringed Trojan helmet. The fur hats of a group of Hassidim were almost as large. I tried to talk to them, but I couldn't get through a coterie bearing USA/ISRAEL AXIS OF RACISM/WHITE SUPREMACY signs. I must rely on my reportorial betters at *The Washington Post:*

> "The Palestinians here in the crowd look at us mistrustfully at first," said Rabbi Yisroel Weiss, 45, of New York. "But then they speak a few words with us, and they show us respect and friendship." . . . He said his group favored dismantling Israel and returning it to the Palestinians.

A sign reading PRO-PALESTINIAN IS NOT ANTI-SEMITIC was carried next to a sign reading SHARON MAKES HITLER PROUD. A delegation of Iranian women in chadors was preceded by a delegation announcing LESBIAN, GAY, BI & TRANS PEOPLE SAY STOP THE WAR. One of the LGBTP was wearing, with panache, a Palestinian flag as a cape. A middle-aged Arab-American man sipped from a Starbucks cup. A college student held a placard: STARBUCKS SUCKS. Enlarged wire-service photos of Palestinian casualties were held aloft, as were THE MEDIA LIES posters. And one banner stated CANNABIS SMOKERS ARE NOT CRIMINALS. A woman ran through the march with a dollar bill dangling from the brim of her baseball cap. On her T-shirt was printed IN PURSUIT OF HAPPINESS.

At the edge of Freedom Plaza a young couple had brought their baby in a stroller and several sheets of cardboard decorated with crossed American and Israeli flags, and slogans: SUPPORT ISRAEL and U.S. AND ISRAEL, BROTHERS UNITED.

"You can't just do nothing," the husband said. Arab-Americans politely ignored them. The rest of the protesters steered away. The only tension on April 20 came from excessive support.

A dozen members of the New Black Panther Party marched (in the military sense) into Freedom Plaza. They were dressed in black fatigues, black motorcycle helmets, and combat boots. They scowled and did drill maneuvers, about-facing and attentioning. The New Black Panthers carried pictures of Saddam Hussein and Osama bin Laden. Their picket signs were professionally printed: THE STATE OF ISRAEL HAS NO RIGHT TO EXIST; THE AMERICAN/ISRAELI WHITE MAN IS THE DEVIL; JIHAD. They hollered, "Death to Israel," "Holy war, holy war, holy war," and "Kill every zionist in Palestine."

For a moment the other demonstrators were silent. They fidgeted. They backed away. "Excuse me, I'm so sorry," said a courteous Arab-American teenager who stepped on my foot. Then a chant began in the crowd: "Killing is not the answer, killing is not the answer." The chant grew louder. Demonstrators raised their fingers in peace signs and began to press in on the New Black Panther Party. Cacophonous drumming came from the Global Justice mobilizers. They shouted, "No more hate!" A woman about my own age began screaming into a bullhorn: "Jews and Arabs unite!" The New Black Panther Party, with somewhat less military élan than before, marched away.

(As it happened, the old Black Panther Party was holding its thirty-fifth reunion that weekend, at the University of the District of Columbia. Former chairman of the party Bobby Seale attended. "I like the methodical way it was done," he was quoted as saying about the war in Afghanistan. "That's how you judge the operation when you're dealing with a bunch of terrorists such as they are.")

The crowd in Freedom Plaza grew and pressed against the front of the National Theatre. Emerging patrons were trapped beneath the marquee. A pair of older women stood patiently, staring at the protesters. "I gather you're not a part of the demonstration," I said.

"No," said one woman, "we came to see a matinee of *Mamma Mia!*"

"But all of America is part of this turmoil," the other woman said.

"How are you going to get out of here?" I asked.

"We'll just go back in," said the first woman, "and see another show."

The Colombia Mobilization joined the ANSWER rally on the Ellipse, and thousands more protesters pushed toward Freedom Plaza. They looked familiar. If I took off my bifocals, they could have been the same denim-pantsed, T-shirted, funny-coifed, oddly shod, beard-attempting kids with whom I'd protested at this very place a generation ago. It was a startling continuity in youthful fashion—as if I'd arrived at my anti–Vietnam War protest in Washington in 1970 and found everyone wearing zoot suits. One thing, however, had changed in thirty-two years. Regular folks felt no desire to kick these young people for the way they looked. The kids were so thoroughly tattooed and body-pierced that, whatever pain someone might want to inflict on them, they'd already inflicted it on themselves.

One bunch began a skit involving a boy in a Halloween skull mask spraying an aerosol can at girls carrying primitive paintings that depicted agricultural endeavors. Then they all dropped dead and yelled something about Colombia.

The marchers trampled the grass on the Ellipse. MORE GARDENS, a sign read. Other posters and banners declared GIVE COMMUNISM A CHANCE; PEACE IS PATRIOTIC; END ASHCROFT'S POLICE STATE; REPUBLICANS FOR PEACE AND JUSTICE FOR ALL; STOP CALLING PALESTINIANS TERRORISTS; REAL PROFITS FROM PEACE; CORPORATIONS ARE KILLING THE WORLD; THE U.S. STARTED IT ALL; DOWN WITH ALGERIAN FASCIST REGIME; PEACE TREATY IN KOREA; LEAVE CHAVEZ ALONE; and FOCUS YOUR DISCONTENT. Indeed.

Many of the signs were wordy: AIDS TREATMENT NOW/COKE'S NEGLECT = DEATH FOR WORKERS IN SOUTH AFRICA. Another began, BUSH'S POX AMERICANA MADE US THE AXIS OF IGNORANCE & A GLOBAL STUPID POWER. THANKS DUBYA . . . and continued in that vein. Some signs were touchingly simple: PLEASE STOP KILLING EVERYBODY. Others had an air of hopelessness: THE ONLY WEAPON A "TERRORIST" NEEDS IS PURPOSE. THEIR PURPOSE GROWS WITH EACH DAY OF THE WAR ON TERROR. One sign, I think, misspoke itself: GOLIATH LOST. David, after all, was an Israeli. The middle-aged "Vermonters for Peace" looked like they gave themselves their own haircuts.

A young lady handed me a square of posterboard washed in pink watercolor with a brighter pink star painted on it and PEACE painstakingly lettered across the front. A family displayed a photograph of Afghan women, labeled "Our Afghan

Sister Family." They gave me a printed handout stating that the Revolutionary Association of the Women of Afghanistan had "condemned the U.S.-backed Northern Alliance for a 'record of human rights violations as bad as that of the Taliban's.'" The handout ended with the sad and deflated sentence: "This statement has apparently been ignored by George Bush and his associates."

A young man wore a T-shirt saying, I USED TO BE A WHITE AMERICAN BUT I GAVE IT UP IN THE INTEREST OF HUMANITY. But another demonstrator wore one of the Abercrombie & Fitch T-shirts that recently had been withdrawn from stores following accusations of racial insensitivity. A fat, slant-eyed bodhisattva appeared above the slogan "Get your Buddha on the Floor." Nearby was a banner from the Buddhist Peace Fellowship.

The four rallies had now joined together, a total of about seventy-five thousand people. They trooped down Pennsylvania Avenue toward the Mall with the Palestinian Solidarity marchers in the lead. Many young Arab-American women had cell phones pressed to their head scarves and were saying things like "You wouldn't believe it, I'm right here on the Mall." Scores of Palestinian flags, and a variety of flags from other Arab nations, were being waved.

"What's *that* flag?" asked another coed being interviewed by Max.

"Lebanon," Max said.

"But why are they waving a flag from *Lebanon*?" she said.

In among the Arab-American families—some of whom had brought coolers and lawn chairs—were college students with a sign reading IF QUEER SOLDIERS UNDERMINE THE MILITARY, SIGN US UP. An exhausted-looking teenager wearing anarchist symbols sat on a curb with a piece of cardboard on which he had lettered BURN ME I'M OLD AND IN THE WAY. Appearing, without intended irony, near the scores of charter buses that had been hired by the demonstrators was VISUALIZE FUEL-EFFICIENT VEHICLES/IT'S A NATIONAL SECURITY ISSUE. Some placards were strangely verbless: HEMP and INTERNATIONAL CRIMINAL COURT. I sent Max to find out why someone was holding up a swath of hot-pink synthetic-mohair cloth. "It's a rallying point for Wesleyan students," said a Wesleyan student in a DEVIANT QUEER T-shirt. At the front of the crowd a banner was being waved—either wholly apposite or completely out of place: SHAME ON DUAL LOYALISTS.

A truck with loudspeakers carried children singing songs of peace. The music was drowned out by young men on another truck with loudspeakers. First they intoned, "The Muslims united / Will never be defeated," and then "Stop the killing / Stop the war." A middle-aged woman dressed as a fairy godmother Rollerbladed between the trucks with a bullhorn. She warbled, "Money for justice, not for bombs. / Money for schools, not guns. / Money for Social Security, too, / When we stop the war," more or less to the tune of "Bibbidity-Bobbidy-Boo" from the Disney cartoon *Cinderella*.

What united these people, other than a general loserish quality? Or maybe it was only that. They've made every question a political question, because in politics—as this political demonstration proved—there is no quality control. But the Arab-Americans didn't look like losers. That's all right. Staking a claim to victimhood has value for even the most successful Americans. Witness Oprah, Rosie, the recent steel tariffs, a farm subsidy bill benefiting vast wheat and cotton plantations, and the complaints of the "sandwich generation" moms pressed in their upper-middle-class lives between the demands of spoiled young children and those of crabby affluent parents. Property rights are to be had in victimhood. Then there is the charm of a good tantrum—familiar to those of us with a three-year-old in the house. The less meliorable the cause of tears, the better the tantrum is. Also, blame negates responsibility. "Who spilled Coca-Cola all over the Third World and crayoned on its walls?" "The World Bank did!" The wonder is not that seventy-five thousand people showed up on April 20, 2002. The wonder is that we all didn't.

The demonstration was fully assembled. Marchers from every participating organization had arrived on the Mall. It was time for the stirring orations. The speakers' platform was ready by the Reflecting Pool, where Martin Luther King, Jr., once stood. But thirty-nine years later it was Cynthia McKinney who strode to the podium. She is the Georgia congresswoman who apologized to Saudi prince Alwaleed bin Talal for Mayor Rudolph Giuliani's refusal of the prince's $10 million check for terrorist victims. She also issued a statement saying, "I am not aware of any evidence showing that President Bush or members of his administration have personally profited from the attacks of 9/11. A complete investigation might reveal that to be the case." And in a speech on recycling she said, "Paper continues to be made from trees."

Representative McKinney called on "people from all walks of life—students, union members, union members on strike, homeless veterans." These were all the walks of life she named. She called on the people in them to do something that I could not hear. The members of the crowd had turned away and begun chatting loudly among themselves. Max and I walked to the Metro. We saw a man who had been on the fringes of various demonstrations all day. He had a sign of his own: GOD PLEASE EVERYONE.

8

THOUGHTS ON THE
EVE OF WAR

❖

Not that I disagreed with everything said by the people who opposed the war with Iraq. As a casus belli, weapons of mass destruction did seem like a pair of pants cut to the size of North Korea and into which Iraq was being stuffed. And claims that Saddam Hussein was cooperating with Osama bin Laden smelled of something found on the Internet late at night along with proof that the Jews and the Rotary Club control the World Bank. What President Bush should have said was "Here's a man who's been murdering everyone he could get his hands on for twenty-five years. We don't need a reason. We're going to do to Iraq's dictator what Hollywood does to its has-beens at the Academy Awards ceremony. We're giving Saddam Hussein a Lifetime Achievement Award."

And I don't blame most nations for not supporting the United States. The world is full of loathsome governments run by criminals, thugs, and beasts. When President Bush mentioned "regime change," hairy little ears pricked up all over the earth. Beads of sweat broke out on low, sloping brows. Bloodstained, grasping hands began to tremble. Poor Colin Powell had to get on the phone to various hyenas in high office and explain to them that America itself was in need of regime change from 1992 to 2000, and we didn't precision-bomb the fellow who was responsible, and we only impeached him a little. Kim Jong Il, Robert Mugabe, and Jacques Chirac should quit worrying. They should look upon Bill Clinton and know the fate that awaits them is a lucrative lecture tour, a big book contract, and many willing, plump young women.

The United Nations Security Council offered a weak and vacillating response to Iraqi provocations. This timidity undermined the power and prestige of the UN—to the profound relief of all thinking people. A potent and esteemed United Nations would be in danger of evolving into a true world government. The individual nations of the earth could become the political equivalents of the individual states of America. Upholding the dignity of the Senate, in these United States of Earth, would be the solons of Turkmenistan, Libya, Sudan, and such, each wielding tremendous power of seniority (since election opponents all conveniently died). Meanwhile, the House of Global Representatives would be given over to debate between rioting Hindus from the Subcontinental delegation and, across the aisle, mainland Chinese chanting in perfect-unison praise of free markets (and the Great Helmsman). The world would have a North Korean secretary of agriculture; a head of the DEA from Cali, Colombia; nine Palestinian suicide bombers on its Supreme Court; an Albanian chairman of the SEC; a dozen warring Liberian joint chiefs of staff; and a French surgeon general telling us we're using too much soap for our health.

We owe a debt of gratitude to the nonaligned countries that opposed the Iraq war. And we owe a debt of gratitude, as well, to our erstwhile allies. We should understand the white-feathered, clucking German response to the prospect of combat in Iraq—understand it for the good thing it is. Germans have turned into poultry with BMWs. What caused this is a mystery, but a splendid mystery given the behavior of Germany in the last century (and, for that matter, since the time of Tacitus). We witness with relief the Boche squawking behind the Rhine, henpecked by even the French. When Germany asks for peace, we are obliged to say, "Yes! Yes! The Versailles Treaty kind!"

And France is a treasure to mankind. French ideas, French beliefs, and French actions form a sort of lodestone for humanity. A moral compass needle needs a butt end. Whatever direction France is pointing—toward collaboration with Nazis, accommodation with communists, existentialism, Jerry Lewis, or UN resolution veto—we can go the other way with a quiet conscience.

9

KUWAIT AND IRAQ

March and April 2003

Why is Iraq so easy to harm and so hard to help? After eight days of war, U.S. troops had arrived at Karbala, sixty miles from Baghdad. Misery had arrived everywhere. But humanitarian relief had gotten only as far as Safwan and Umm Qasr, just across the border from Kuwait.

I could see one reason that relief had gone no farther. I was outside Safwan on March 28, on the roof of a Kuwait Red Crescent tractor-trailer full of food donations. Below, a couple of hundred shoving, shouldering, kneeing, kicking Iraqi men and boys were grabbing at boxes of food.

Red Crescent volunteers provided the boxes, gingerly, to the mob. Each white carton would be grasped by three or four or five belligerents and pulled in three or four or five directions—tug-of-Congolese-civil-war.

Every person in the mob seemed to be arguing with every other person. Giving in to conflicting impulses to push themselves forward and pull others away, shouting Iraqis were propelled in circles. A short, plump, bald man sank in the roil. A small boy, red-faced and crying, was crushed between two bellowing fat men. An old man was trampled trying to join the fray.

The Iraqis were snatching the food as if they were starving, but they couldn't have been starving or they wouldn't have been able to snatch so well. Most looked fully fed. Some were *too* fit and active. Everyone behind the trailer was expending a lot of calories at noon on a ninety-degree day.

Looking out, I saw irrigated patches in the desert, at about the same density as the patches on the uniform of a mildly diligent Boy Scout. The tomatoes were ripe. Nannies, billies, and kids browsed between garden plots. Goat Bolognese was on offer, at least for some locals.

There was no reason for people to clobber one another. Even assuming that each man in the riot—and each boy— was the head of a family, and assuming the family was huge, there was enough food in the truck. Mohammed al-Kandari, a doctor from the Kuwait Red Crescent Society, had explained this to the Iraqis when the trailer arrived. Al-Kandari was a forceful explainer. He resembled a beneficent version of Bluto in the Popeye comics, or Bluto in *Animal House.*

Al-Kandari had persuaded the Iraqis to form ranks. They looked patient and grateful, the way we privately imagine the recipients of food donations looking when we're writing checks to charities. Then the trailer was opened, and everything went to hell.

Al-Kandari marched through the donnybrook and slammed the trailer doors shut. He harangued the Iraqis. They lined up again. The trailer was opened, and everything went to hell.

Al-Kandari waded in and closed the trailer doors again. He swung his large arms in parallel arcs at the Iraqis. "Line up!" he boomed; "Queue!" he thundered—the Arabic-speaking doctor speaking to Arabic speakers in English, as if no Arabic word existed for the action.

Al-Kandari took a pad of Post-it notes and a marker pen from his lab-coat pocket. "Numbers!" he said, still speaking English. "I will give you all numbers!" A couple of hundred shouldering, shoving Iraqi men and boys grabbed at the Post-it notes.

The doctor gave up and opened the trailer doors. I climbed the ladder behind the truck cab to get a better view.

Aid-seekers in England would queue automatically by needs, disabled war vets and nursing mothers first. Americans would bring lawn chairs and sleeping bags, camp out the night before, and sell their places to the highest bidders. The Japanese would text-message one another, creating virtual formations, getting in line to get in line. Germans would await commands from a local official, such as the undersupervisor of the town clock. Even Italians know how to line up, albeit in an ebullient wedge. The happier parts of the world have capacities for self-organization so fundamental and obvious that they appear to be the pillars of civilization. But here—on the road to Ur, in the Tigris-Euphrates Valley, where civilization has obtained for five thousand years longer than it has, for example, at a Libertarian Party confab in Phoenix—nothing was supporting the roof.

What I saw, however, wasn't anarchy. British soldiers stood nearby, emirs of everything within rifle shot. The Iraqis did not use weapons or even fists in the aid scramble. Later a British soldier said, "We try to stay out of crowd control, because it looks like we're trying to stop the aid distribution. But we can't let them start fighting." They did start fighting. A few Iraqis hit each other with sticks. They fought, however, at the front end of the truck. British soldiers broke it up.

The Iraqis didn't try to climb into the tractor-trailer or break through its side doors. Red Crescent volunteers, coming and going from the back of the truck, were unmolested. Once an aid box was fully in an Iraqi's control and had been pulled free from the commotion, no one tried to take it. I saw four boxes being guarded by a seven-year-old boy.

I watched a confident gray-haired man push toward the trailer gate. He had wire-rimmed glasses on the end of his nose and a cigarette in the corner of his mouth. He dove for a box, his glasses flying, the cigarette embers burning various *gutra* headdresses and *dishdashah* skirts. He disappeared for the better part of a minute. Then he came out on the other side of the throng, box under one arm and glasses somehow back on his face (but minus the cigarette). The gray-haired man looked around and delivered an open-handed whack to someone who, I guess, had indulged in a late hit.

I stared at the rampage for an hour. Now and then I'd be noticed on the trailer roof. Whenever I caught someone's eye, I was greeted with a big, happy smile. The Iraqis were having fun.

Worse fun was to follow. We were out in the countryside because the first aid convoy to Safwan, two days before, had gone into the center of town and had been looted in a less orderly riot. I left the truck roof and interviewed al-Kandari, or tried to. The doctor was still being importuned for worthless numbers on Post-it notes. "We almost get organized," he overstated, "but then some gangs will come from downtown, by running or by truck." They were arriving already, in anything they could get to move—taxis, pickups, ancient Toyota Land Cruisers, bicycles, Russian Belarus tractors, a forklift, a dump truck.

The men from town promptly climbed into the Red Crescent truck. They threw boxes to their buddies. The volunteers fled. In a few minutes one squad of looters had seventeen aid boxes. The box throwers were dancing and singing in the back of the tractor-trailer. A reporter who'd covered the previous convoy said, "I saw these same guys." He pointed to a wolfish-looking fellow who was pulling the tail of his *gutra* across his face. "You can tell the really bad ones," the reporter said. "They have shoes."

Al-Kandari ordered the driver to start the truck. The British troops cleared the highway. The truck drove back to Safwan with the trailer doors open and looters still inside. The other looters, in their miscellany of rides, gave chase. Men stood on car hoods and in pickup beds, trying to catch boxes being thrown from inside the trailer. Boxes fell, spraying fruit, rice, and powdered milk across the pavement. A flatbed truck passed us, piled with scores of aid boxes. The men standing on the bumpers had shoes. Horn-honking, chanting, and other noises of celebration could be heard in the distance.

We drove through Safwan. Boys ran alongside our convoy, managing, with deft coordination of purposes, to jeer and beg at the same time. A reporter tossed a bottle of water to a boy. The boy picked it up and threw it at the reporter.

Safwan's houses, placed higgledy-piggledy, were built of tumbling-down mud brick. The other buildings were squat and lumpish, their walls formed of concrete with too much aggregate in the mix—Baath Party adobe. Signs of economic activity were nil. In the one park, playground equipment was rusty and broken. Trash was everywhere. Hundreds of black plastic shopping sacks blew along the streets, snagging in the rest of the rubbish. The people of Iraq may have had nothing, but they had the bag it came in.

Safwan was a dump, but not a ruin. There was little war damage. Coalition forces had destroyed almost nothing but the customs sheds, which hadn't been used since 1991, when the Gulf War cease-fire was signed—as it happened, at Safwan.

In an hour and a half we were back in Kuwait City—in the same geography, on the same oil reserves, with the same people, same language, same religion. But Kuwait City is Houston without Enron (or, unfortunately, beer).

Twelve years ago Kuwait City was a dump *and* a ruin. The Iraqis destroyed what they couldn't steal and left the rubble full of their garbage, including piles of human feces. The hotel where the Gulf War press stayed survived only because it had carpets made from some self-extinguishing synthetic fiber. The Iraqis kept pouring diesel oil on the carpets. The flames kept going out. The hotel stank. There was no electricity. The rooftop cisterns ran dry. The only food was eggs, cooked by the hotel staff over campfires in the parking lot.

Twelve years later in Kuwait City I had tea and smoked salmon sandwiches and tarts and cakes and sticky treats with an American lawyer who has lived in Kuwait for twenty years. He was trapped by the 1990 invasion and forced to hide. He described the convoy of empty trucks that came from Baghdad every day—"all kinds of trucks, dump trucks included"—and returned every night full of swag. He told about the Baghdad buses that were driven to Kuwait carrying members of the "People's Army"—men and women turned loose in the shopping districts to pull down gates, push in doors, and loot. "The Iraqis," he said, "pried up the reflectors between the lanes in the streets and took them back to Baghdad." Then the lawyer spread his hands to take in the magnificence of the restaurant where we were sitting. "Even after all that," he said, "there was a lot left in Kuwait."

The smelly Gulf War hotel and everything else I remembered had been rebuilt or replaced. Freedom accomplishes extraordinary things. And there is an extraordinary list of things that Kuwait is free of. Kuwait is free of the Wahhabi religious idealism that inspires neighboring Saudi Arabia. There is an evangelical church in Kuwait City, a Coptic church, and a Roman Catholic Holy Family cathedral complex with crosses forty feet high on its gable ends. (I confess to thinking that one way to get a drink in Kuwait was to take communion. But a priest from India drank all the wine.)

Kuwait is free of the lofty goals of pan-Arab socialism that animate the Baath Party. Kuwait is also free of the lofty goals that animate other political parties. Political parties are illegal. To vote in Kuwait one must be basically a son of a family that lived there when oil was something that seeped from the ground and ruined the camel forage. Franchise is denied to women and to most naturalized citizens and to the 62.9 percent of Kuwait's population—mostly guest workers and their dependents—who aren't citizens at all. The national assembly is of dubious political power anyway. Kuwait is more majority-owned than majority-ruled. The relatives of Sheik Jaber al-Ahmed al-Sabah have held control since the eighteenth century.

As a nation, Kuwait has been, arguably, free of freedom itself. Claimed in turn by Constantinople, Riyadh, and Baghdad, Kuwait has survived by playing Turks off Persians, Arabs off one another, and the English off everyone. Kuwait became a British protectorate in 1899. In 1961 the British were asked to leave and immediately asked to return, to forestall an invasion by a previous Iraqi strongman, Abd al-Karim Qasim.

Now, some would say, Kuwait is an American fief. The Kuwaitis are free of resentment about that. Being an American in Kuwait City was like being a minor celebrity come back home to live. Walking through the souks, I was greeted with shy smiles and hellos from fellow shoppers. Merchants invited me to have coffee *after* I'd bought something. In the luggage souk two shopkeepers left their stores and showed me around until I'd bought what I wanted from a rival. The teller at the bank told me he liked my haircut. As the war neared, hotels and shopping centers put metal detectors inside their doors. As I was going into the Salhiya Mall, a security guard saw me start to empty the many pockets of my safari jacket. He got up, helped me out of the coat, carried it around the detector stanchions unsearched, and helped me put it back on.

The freedom that Kuwaitis do have is the freedom to do what they want. What they want to do is shop, eat, and sit around. The Kuwaitis are among the few peoples on earth— teenagers aside—who don't sneer at these freedoms. Apparently, they never did. Kuwait's Popular Traditional Museum is devoted to recapturing "Old Kuwait"—"old" being before 1951, when bountiful oil revenues arrived. In the museum's corridors are life-size models of bazaars, food markets, coffeehouses, kitchens, and home interiors, all filled with mannequins in period dress, sitting around. Exhibited artifacts include early electric fans, gramophones, Brownie cameras, radios with vacuum tubes, and a set of china commemorating the 1937 coronation of George VI.

In the new Kuwait this freedom of ways and means benefits from means that are prodigious. The McDonald's on Arabian Gulf Street has a doorman and a maître d'. A Mercedes dealership on the west side of town is the size of a county fair. Premium gasoline costs eighty-seven cents a gallon or—to put that in Kuwaiti currency (at $3.34 to the dinar)—nothing. Lunch lasts from noon to five. The *gutra* on the man in line ahead of me at the McDonald's bore the Dunhill label.

Souk Sharq, on Kuwait Bay near the sheik's palace, might have been designed by Frank Lloyd Wright, if Wright had been alive in 2000 and in need of a quick job to knock off. The souk has its own yacht harbor. Inside the marketplace is a wide central aisle, space that in an American shopping center would be given over to booths selling sunglasses and caps with sports-team logos. At Souk Sharq one aisle stall was occupied by the De Beers diamond company.

As previously noted, Kuwait is not as wealthy as Luxembourg, on paper. But the papers at Souk Sharq's newsstand were censored (although it was décolletage, rather than economic information, that was blacked out with marker pens). Anyway, Luxembourgers may be better at earning, but they cannot excel the Kuwaitis at spending.

The souk's grocery store, the Sultan Center, was Balducci's as Costco. Caviar tins were piled to the ceiling. In the food court the Chinese counter had Peking duck to go. At a children's clothing store a toddler play outfit—shirt, jumper, and gym shoes—came to $140 worth of jam mop and chocolate milk sponge. The Kookaï boutique was filled with the latest in the fashionable ethnic look; never mind that Kuwaitis *are* ethnics.

I interviewed a Bedouin the next day. He was tending his camel herd in the desert west of the city. He wore sandals and a sail-sized *dishdashah*. His *gutra* (not from Dunhill) was tucked in manifold gatherings under the *agal* headband. On the back of the Bedouin's riding camel was a carved-wood and tooled-leather footstool of a saddle. The camel's flanks were covered by vividly woven and elaborately tasseled wool provision bags. This was the first time I'd ever seen anyone really use the kind of handicrafts that tourists bring home. The Bedouin milked a mother camel and offered me the bowl. We sat around. He said, "I have three sons in medical school in the United States."

The camel's milk was frothy, light, slightly sweet. It would make an excellent latte. The desert sky was crosshatched with power lines. Pumping stations and tank farms could be seen in the distance. There was a six-lane highway behind the desert patriarch. He was Lawrence of New Jersey.

The liberties of Kuwait may be quotidian, but Kuwaitis are serious about them. Even in New Jersey the right to drive isn't exercised with Kuwaiti vigor. I was on that six-lane highway going seventy miles an hour in the left-hand lane, in bumper-to-bumper traffic, when a Mercedes 500SE sedan blinked its lights behind me. I had nowhere to go. The Mercedes driver cut left onto the unpaved shoulder and proceeded at ninety or a hundred down the barely car-width slot between the traffic and the concrete barrier. I could see his taillights wobble. He was terraplaning, gravel-surfing, leaving a mile of stone stars in the windshields of the cars ahead.

The small, ordinary freedoms of life are priceless, especially if you remember to have someone else pay the price. Billboards on the backs of Kuwait's city buses show a photograph of a Kuwaiti hugging an American soldier during the 1991 liberation with the caption, in English and Arabic, "We Never Forget."

In early March 2003 most American soldiers were too far from town to be hugged. Also, they were about to liberate in the other direction. I wondered whether the Iraqis would say, "We never forget." If so, in what tone of voice will they say it?

Two days before the war began, the president of the United States gave an inspirational speech.

"I thought the Bush speech was a little bit inspiring," said a PFC at an Army Aviation Chinook helicopter base in western Kuwait.

"Nothing we didn't expect, just a confirmation," a warrant officer said.

"We most definitely have more to look forward to, now, instead of the standstill wait," said a sergeant. She'd obtained, somehow, in a Muslim marketplace, a case of pork sausages, and she was cooking lunch for her platoon in scrounged pans over a jury-rigged propane fire.

"This is just like being home after work," said a platoon member. "We're enjoying ourselves while we can. It's going to be a longer day once combat begins."

Some of the battalion's troops had come from Afghanistan. Kuwait's landscape was bleaker still. Six sandbags on the floor of each portable toilet—more ballast than portable toilets are given at Ozfest—said everything about the wind. The soldiers had free weights, laptops (though no Internet access), and once-a-week phone calls home. They said they had CDs with a variety of music: country, heavy metal, rap, bluegrass, gospel, alternative rock. But each soldier listened to one variety, not to the others. There was no "Tenting Tonight" or "Lili Marlene" in the Walkman-headphone army. "Everything is fine, aside from cold showers," said a private.

"One day closer to redeployment," said a lieutenant.

"Your worst day of waiting is better than your best day of combat," said a captain.

Asked about world opinion, peace protests, the UN, and so forth, a helicopter pilot said, "I don't care. We're here to do one thing and one thing only. If they tell me to go hurt someone, I'll go hurt someone."

That was a chilling statement of military professionalism, unless it was a heartwarming testimony to what military professionalism means in a democracy with armed forces under civilian control. Either way, the professionalism was different than it was in Kipling's time. A second pilot, leaving base as a sandstorm blew in, said to the first, "If I don't come back, I'm willing you all my tampons."

"We came here to do a job," said an enlisted man. "It doesn't matter what we think about it, we've got to do it." Then he added, "I'm doing it for my wife and kids."

And each soldier may have been listening to different music, but all the soldiers were *not* listening to the same tunes. A member of the popular country-and-western group the Dixie Chicks had stated that President Bush made her ashamed to be from Texas. A gunnery officer collected Dixie Chicks CDs to throw out the window of his Chinook. Also a campaign was discussed to return the Statue of Liberty to the French: "Take the Bitch Back."

The previous week a network anchorman had been scheduled to take a ride on one of the battalion's helicopters. I had happened to be on the base. I asked the private on sentry duty at the landing pad, "Have you seen Peter Jennings?"

"No, sir," said the private. "And I don't much like him, anyway."

At Camp Virginia, in northern Kuwait, amenities were fewer. Hot meals were infrequent. There were long lines for those cold showers. A sergeant took me for a ride in his Bradley fighting vehicle. We went across the desert at terrific speed— "terrific" being about forty-five mph. But in a large armored, tracked vehicle, this is like forty-five mph down the stairs on a cafeteria tray. As we crested a berm, the sergeant said, "Sometimes I don't know why they pay me!" He'd been in Kuwait for six months. Camp Virginia came back into view. "And sometimes," the sergeant said, "they couldn't pay me enough."

His crew wanted to know about *my* pay. "How much do

you get paid to come here?" they asked. "Is this fun for you?"
An officer from Army Public Affairs shushed them.

I was shown a mobile command-post tent carried by
five trucks and big enough for a circus that's given up aerial
acts. But inside, it seemed to be a Wall Street bond-trading
boiler room. Officers sat at rows of tables, staring at
computer terminals. In front of the tables were PowerPoint
presentations on three large screens. Map displays showed
enemy and coalition military positions in the planned initial combat zone, in Iraq as a whole, and in the entire Middle
East.

The tent was windowless, the better to protect against
NBC (nuclear, biological, chemical) threats. The other tents
were also windowless. Ordinary soldiers, along with headquarters staff, spend a lot of on-duty time staring at computer
terminals. And they spend a lot of time inside NBC suits,
behind gas-mask lenses, breathing through filters. In the back
of the Bradley fighting vehicle, where six combat infantry-
men sit, the only peek at the outside is through periscopic
slits. The Chinooks themselves, if you stand away from the
door gunner's post, don't have a view. Or they don't unless
the crew drops the rear-loading ramp. Then you have the
disconcerting view you'd get from putting a French window
in the floor of your mountaintop house deck. There's something as indoorsy as eBay about the twenty-first-century
military. And from all I know about either part of that simile,
something as historically transformative.

The military is indoorsy but not homey. The numerous
ducts, tubes, and wiring bundles of technology—covered by
Sheetrock and acoustic tile in civilian life—are left bare in
the Army. The hardware seems to expand with exposure.
Austere functionality has so overgrown the interior of the

Humvee that only four soldiers can fit into that hulking vehicle. Perhaps technology is squeezing humans out of warfare. But will they want to go?

A Chinook helicopter crew took me along on a live-fire exercise, to practice with the door-mounted M-60 machine gun. We flew to a range on the northern Kuwait border where Iraqi military junk from the Gulf War had been hauled. One of every so many rounds in the M-60's ammunition belt magazine was a tracer, which left a Fourth of July rocket trail telling where the bullets were going. I asked if it was like shooting a rifle, aiming precisely, or like shooting a shotgun, leading the target. "It's better than either," said the gunnery officer who'd been collecting Dixie Chicks CDs. "It's like walking the dog!" Bullets ambled along toward a Soviet-era Iraqi tank—trot, trot, trot, and mess in the yard.

Flying back from the firing range, I had a moment of clarity about one of the supposed underlying causes of the conflict in Iraq. The Kuwait desert is as flat as a patio and as big as Connecticut and Rhode Island combined. The entire space appeared to be covered in tanks, artillery pieces, Bradley fighting vehicles, Humvees, transport trucks, and Patriot missile batteries. Streaks of asphalt runway ran in all directions. The tarmac held fighter planes, cargo planes, and hundreds more helicopters: Chinooks, Black Hawks, Apaches, Kiowas. Amid the matériel were Camp Virginia, Camp New York, Camp Pennsylvania, and—the way it looked to me—Camps Other Forty-seven and Camp Puerto Rico and Camp Guam. Military force extended from me to the horizon in every direction, 360 degrees of war. It is much cheaper to buy oil than to steal it.

* * *

At dawn on Thursday, March 20, when the first American missiles struck Baghdad, I was asleep in a big, soft bed. My wife, watching late-night news in the United States, called me in Kuwait to tell me the war had started. That was embarrassing for a professional journalist in a combat zone. But I looked around my comfortable hotel room and thought, "We *are* fighting for freedom. In this case, the freedom to go back to sleep in a big, soft bed."

I got out of bed, eventually, and went to interview the random bystanders who have become central to news coverage in the contemporary era. About a third of the stores and businesses in Kuwait City were closed. A bomb-sniffing police dog was digging furiously in a concrete planter outside my hotel, which would have been alarming if the dog hadn't had the unmistakable mien of a pooch who smells something deliciously dead.

The Kuwaitis I talked to were confident and enthusiastic. The proprietor of a fabric shop said, "America is here. I feel no problem in Kuwait."

I went to buy additional pens and notebooks, in case other spokesmen for the Arab street were more loquacious. I asked the stationery-store owner about the onset of hostilities. "This is good," he said. "This is better. I want Saddam finish." He told me about seeing a young Filipina raped by Iraqi troops in 1990, outside his shop door. "I could do nothing," he said. "They loot my store—everything." He put a finger to his temple. "Click," he said. He all but came over the counter with angry enthusiasm. He declared, "I go for a soldier!" Then he sighed. "But my son says, 'You are sixty-seven.'" His Indian shop assistant steered me away from the less expensive pens.

Non-Kuwaiti guest workers were less certain about the war (although the stationery-store assistant did give me a hug after I'd interviewed his boss—and bought two boxes of felt-tips and a dozen steno pads).

"My owner won't let me close," said a Pakistani man at an appliance store. "You ask me, I close. Maybe you will inform him."

The Indian manager of a women's clothing store said, "I think this is not fair. Is for us and everybody, not good. Is bad for Saddam Hussein and very sad because of one person is all this trouble."

"You mean because of Saddam Hussein?" I asked.

"Yes, Saddam."

"But you still don't think this war is good."

"Yes."

I questioned a Filipino clerk at a photo-developing booth about his decision to come to work.

Me: Some businesses are closed.
Clerk: Sometimes they do not open.
Me: But you're open. You're not afraid?
Clerk: Some are a little afraid.
Me: How do you feel about the bombing?
Clerk: (Polite smile.)
Me: The U.S. bombed Baghdad this morning.
Clerk: I did not know about this. (Another polite smile.)

Iraq began firing missiles at Kuwait. Only the first air-raid warning had any effect on the Kuwaitis. When the sirens started, I saw a man in a *dishdashah* come out of an office building and rush nervously toward his car. Fifteen feet from the vehicle he stopped and pressed the door-lock button on his key-chain remote, and then he went back into the office building.

There was a mannequin wearing a gas mask in a store's window display, but it turned out that the store sold equipment to the police and military. Plastic sheeting and duct tape were displayed in the hardware souk. "Many sales," said a fellow at one of the stalls. "But not because of the war—because of good price."

One of the Kuwaiti soldiers guarding my hotel wanted America to pick up the pace. "Tomorrow, tomorrow, and tomorrow," he exhorted, and made the motion of a baseball umpire calling a runner safe. "Boom!" he urged.

A tiny old lady wrapped in a black *abayah* approached me in the vegetable souk. She had the face of Mother Teresa— or, rather, the face that Mother Teresa deserved but didn't get. "American?" she asked.

"Yes," I said.

She gave me a beatific grin, a smile of hope and blessing, and drew her finger across her throat. "*Saddam!*" she beamed.

There was no sign of fear or patience among the Kuwaitis, any more than there would be among the Iraqis at Safwan. Sermons could be preached about the civilizing benefits and progressive influences of fear and patience.

And I've preached all of them to my three- and six-year-old daughters. I suspect I have one or two elements of the Muslim world in my own home.

But only one or two. An article in *Kuwait This Month* featured the *miswak,* a twig from the saltbrush tree that is employed as a natural toothbrush. "Muslims use it," the article said, "on the recommendations of Prophet Muhammad."

The Prophet is quoted in the text: "Use the *miswak,* for verily, it purifies the mouth, and it is a pleasure for the Lord." Not only is there no separation of Church and State in the Muslim world, there is no separation of Church and dental hygiene.

In *Arab Times,* a Kuwait English-language daily, the law court roundup reported that "S.H.F." was accused of raping "O.S.M." He took her to an apartment for a tryst, then invited some other men to have sex with her. She refused and was raped. S.H.F. was acquitted. The court ruled that "the testimony of the victim cannot be taken into account because during earlier interrogation she had said S.H.F. had sex with her three times and later confessed to having sex five times."

But just when I had decided that the people of the Middle East were as troublesome and confusing as the algebra they invented, there came a glimpse of the brotherhood of mankind, or—apropos of algebra—the brotherhood of sophomoric guykind. I was in a phone store when a young Kuwaiti married couple came in. They were in their late teens. She was a beauty, though cloaked to the soles of her feet and veiled to the eyes. A girl who is really pretty—whether she wraps herself in an *abayah,* a nun's habit, or the front hall rug—never wraps herself so that the world can't tell. The boy was tall and gawky and had a foolish grin. A line of hickeys ran up his neck.

The night I returned from Safwan, a missile hit the Souk Sharq. The Kuwaitis claimed it was a "Seersucker" missile. Who names these things—leftover old preppies at the CIA? Next we'll have the Madras Cummerbund missile and the Lime Green Pants with Little Trout Flies missile. I went to Souk Sharq in the morning. Kuwaiti police officers were lifting the crime-scene tape so that all the other fellows could have a look at the cool destruction.

The damage wasn't great. But in one perfume shop every bottle had been exploded by the warhead's shock wave. The place reeked of Shalimar. A mature adult American with a perfume store would have been on his cell phone screaming at his insurance agent. The Kuwaiti store owner was sitting in a chair sipping a little cup of coffee. I introduced myself. The owner pointed cheerfully to the wet pile of broken glass. "Special price!" he said.

Being a "unilateral" reporter in Kuwait, rather than a reporter "embedded" with the military, meant that, like everyone else, I watched the war on TV. Except I was too close for comfort—to TV, not war. Cable and broadcast networks had taken over swaths of Kuwait's hotels. I was walking down the hall in the Sheraton and saw a huddle of serious-faced ABC television producers. They were having an animated discussion. Something was up. I moved closer.

"Do you think we should wake Diane?"

"I don't want to wake Diane."

"Maybe we shouldn't wake Diane."

I started to keep a notebook of things said by people who were sitting behind desks on television:

CNN, 3/19, Larry King to John Major: "I don't think the United States has ever started a war."

CNN, 3/20, several hours after the "decapitation strike" against Saddam Hussein: "It is like a brief intermission in some terrible, but real, movie."

CNN, 3/23, concerning a 101st Airborne soldier who threw a grenade into an officer's tent: "We'd like to point out that the soldier is said to have an Arab- or Muslim-sounding last name, but we'd like to point out that at this time this doesn't mean anything at all."

But I gave it up. I'm not prejudiced against CNN. It was just the first station on my hotel-room channel changer.

Every so often, the unilateral reporters were sent on official minibus tours, such as the one to Safwan. Thirty-five or forty journalists would pack into the minibus, pressed against the windows like pickles in a jar. The tours were arranged by the Kuwaiti Ministry of Information. The MOI falls under the purview of Kuwait's Department of Moral Guidance and Public Relations, and *there* is a branch of government that's a boat with two sterns and a big Evinrude on each.

The minibuses made a lot of unexplained stops in the desert. At each stop a small, bossy man from the Ministry of Information shouted through a bullhorn: "Everybody get back on the buses."

Nobody got back on the buses.

"We are leaving," shouted the little bossy man.

We didn't leave.

I went to Umm Qasr, Iraq's only deepwater port. I saw Iraq's least successful looter scurrying down a side street clutching a vacuum cleaner hose, a strip of rubber molding, and the kind of small, dirty throw rug you don't mind if the dog chews. I saw Umm Qasr's port facilities. They'd been looted. Umm Qasr was the site of a detention facility for several thousand Iraqi "enemy prisoners of war," or "EPWs" ("POW" having, apparently, acquired too much political cachet for use on Iraqis). We were driven by the detention facility so fast that we couldn't see anything, because, we were told, under the

Geneva Convention, prisoners of war are not allowed to be exhibited to the press.

I was also going to keep a notebook of my own thoughts about the war:

- Decapitation strike. Cut head off dinosaur. Dinosaurs have brains the size of walnuts. Leaves a lot of thrashing stegosaurus.
- Was U.S. radio reporter on roof of Nagasaki Hilton in 1945 saying, "Civilian casualties are going to cause problems for the U.S. winning the hearts and minds of the Japanese people"?
- Military bans embed satellite phones. Iraqis listening in. Getting toward April 15. Iraqis asking, "Is this H and R bloc a new coalition?"
- Ph.D. dissertation to be written about the relationship of twenty-four-hour war coverage to reality TV. Glad I'm not in grad school.
- Will Boston Pops give concert featuring TV networks' "War in Iraq" theme music?
- Geraldo expelled for sketching U.S. positions in sand on live TV. Given Geraldo investigative journalism track record, resulted in Iraqi artillery pounding Damascus.

But I gave that up, too. Geraldo appeared at my hotel, looking dramatically dirty and accompanied by enough equipment and crew to reinvade Iraq. With the Pentagon's blessing, he soon did. "The troops like him," an Army public affairs officer explained. And why not? Geraldo is courageous, patriotic, and without him the troops aren't on TV.

Besides, a reporter didn't have to be foolishly brave to feel like a fool during the war. Thousands of Kuwaiti citizens and residents were imprisoned in Iraq in 1990 and 1991. Six hundred and five are still unaccounted for. Kuwait's National Committee for Missing and Prisoner of War Affairs held a reception for POW families and the press. Solemn and formally dressed Kuwaitis presented journalists, who were almost as grubby as Geraldo, with yellow roses, lapel pins, POW/MIA banners, and letters written by family members. One was from "A Daughter of a POW" and was addressed "To the whole world . . . to everyone who live on our good and blessed earth."

Tables of food had been set out. Waiters circulated with glasses of fruit juice. The room was decorated with the yellow ribbons that have gone—in good-thief-on-cavalry fashion—from self-pitying refrain in a country-and-western prison song to international symbol of hope and remembrance. There was no tactful way to escape interviewing the families.

I was with a Lebanese journalist friend who offered to translate. He guided me to two sisters wearing yards of stiff, shiny black cloth, Mona and Naaima. "They're Bedouin women," my friend said, "from a very humble background. You can tell by how dark they are from the sun. This is the only place you'd see them mix with wealthy Kuwaitis." Mona and Naaima's three brothers, ages nineteen to twenty-four, were arrested by the Iraqis in 1990.

"Why were they arrested?" I asked.

"They were in the Kuwait Army," said Mona. Naaima was arrested, too. She was a nurse. The Iraqis asked her to work in a hospital in Iraq. She refused and was sent to prison for four months, first in Basra, then in Najaf, then in Karbala. Her daughter was seven months old. The girl, now a thirteen-year-old in jeans, was at the reception with her mother and aunt. Naaima hadn't known that her brothers were held in the same prison she was. She caught a glimpse of them as she was being moved from Basra to Najaf. Three years ago Mona spoke with a former POW who recalled seeing her eldest brother in prison in 1991. That was all they knew.

"I'm the scum of the earth," I said to my Lebanese friend. "Our business eats these things. We're maggots in people's grief. And we can't even keep a story like this in the news for more than one *Oprah* episode. There's nothing I can do. There's worse than nothing. I'm a beacon of false hope, a Cape Hatteras lighthouse in downtown Raleigh." Or I said something like that, probably not so carefully thought out.

My friend spoke to the two women. They looked at me with concern and said something in Arabic. "They are firm believers in Allah," my friend said. "Whatever their brothers' fate is, they're willing to accept it, knowing that their brothers served Kuwait and served it well."

Baghdad fell. Iraqi rioting commenced. Looting was undertaken in earnest. Twenty-four-hour television coverage turned into the Shopping Channel. The war was over—not the killing, dying part but the part in which I was involved. I could tell by a sign on the bulletin board at the Kuwaiti Ministry of Information press center: FOR SALE—HELMET, U.S. ARMY MEDIUM, LIKE NEW, $100. FLAK VEST, CONCEALABLE, WORN ONCE, $350.

Newscasters began mentioning the Laci Peterson murder case. Some attributed the lapsing scrutiny of the war to the short attention span of the American public. But many

Americans have given their all—indeed, could be said to have sacrificed their lives—doing their best for people who now hate them. A nation that has teens in the house can't be expected to focus on Iraq forever.

On April 16 I hitched a ride on an Air Force C-17 cargo plane to the Baghdad airport. Bouncing around in the windowless cargo hold was an Oshkosh fire engine.

"A fire engine?" said the Army public affairs officer who took charge of me in Baghdad, and whom I'll call Major Bob. "We've already got a fire engine. What we need is water to put in it."

Thousands of troops occupied the airport. Their water was in one-liter plastic bottles. Sometimes there was a little water left over from drinking. Then a shower could be had by poking holes in the bottom of the water bottle, holding it right side up, and unscrewing the cap.

Hot meals were unavailable. The Meals Ready to Eat are less of a death penalty to the digestive system than they were during the Gulf War, and more of a life sentence to the school lunchroom. The weather was hot and windy in the daytime and hot and windy at night.

Troops and supplies were being flown into the airport's cargo facilities. The passenger terminal, designed by French architects in a "Harrah's Arabia" style, was being used as a bivouac. The combination of no planes at the gates, dull food, nonfunctioning air-conditioning, and snoring people stretched out on uncomfortable boarding-lounge furniture made for a shock of the familiar to a frequent flyer. Except you could smoke. Except everyone was running out of cigarettes.

There was an ad on the airport wall for the place where Iraq's information minister, Mohammed Saeed al-Sahhaf, used to regale the international press: "Al Rashid—It's More than a Hotel."

"It's a target," an Army captain said.

I camped in the airport's administration building, in an office with bookshelves full of Reagan-era Boeing manuals and out-of-date Jeppeson guides to takeoff and landing patterns at international airports. I did not find one for La Guardia with the World Trade Center towers circled in red. What I found instead was culture, or evidence of it.

Looting by Americans was strictly forbidden. But scrounging was okay, and we didn't have coffee cups. The Iraqi airport administrators had a wall of personal lockers, all carefully locked but with doors subject to persuasion by a Leatherman tool. I found a cup in one locker and—along with a bag of loose tea, a sliver of soap, and a spare pair of socks—the crudely printed cover of an English-language Iraqi edition of *Waiting for Godot*.

Artistic genius, arguably including Samuel Beckett's, has limned the extraordinary experiences of war—terror, desperation, suffering, bravery. Banal discomforts, however, need less brilliant insights to convey them. For example, "sandstorm." The word is too beach, too playground. And Iraq doesn't have sand. It has fine-ground goat droppings and minute particles of gluey clay. When the wind whips up, it's small-craft warnings in the lizard terrarium, a horizontal dirt blizzard. Then the drizzle that comes with spring sandstorms in the Persian Gulf begins, and with every breath the soldiers are fed a slime pie. Months of that and the food and the water, plus those extraordinary experiences of war, such as getting shot at, are wearing.

The lavatory facilities at the airport administration building consisted of one plastic stacking conference room chair with a hole cut out of the seat. It was placed over a bucket behind the TO BAGHDAD sign on the departure ramp.

The soldiers guarding a presidential palace near the airport had been in the gulf since the previous July. Their lieutenant had been killed in the war. A sergeant said that his wife, unable to get a babysitter, had taken their five-year-old daughter to the lieutenant's funeral in the United States. "One of Daddy's soldiers is on his way to heaven," his wife explained.

"You mean he died," said the little girl. When they got home, the girl took a tablet and pencil and went into her bedroom. The sergeant often receives elaborate scribbles in the mail. Half an hour later his daughter came out and said, "Usually I write Daddy, but you'll have to write this so he can understand it: 'Daddy, be safe. Come home in one piece.'"

Another soldier was carrying a chrome-plated Winged Victory in his pocket. His thirteen-year-old son's soccer team had won the league championship. His son broke the "angel" off the top of the trophy and sent it with a note: "This will protect you."

Sergeant Luis Cubera was a New York City emergency medical technician. Major Bob said, "He was in Tower One when Tower Two got hit."

"It gave me a reason to come back in the Army," said Sergeant Cubera.

The palace was called, I think, Abu Griab, but Iraq's presidential palaces are marked with barbed wire and watchtowers, not park service signs or historical plaques. The palace was built on an artificial island in a fishpond big enough for waterskiing. There was a swamped speedboat in the shallows. Some soldiers had removed whip antennas from Humvees and rigged the antennas with communication wire and safety pins. A fish fry was planned.

The palace architecture hinted that Iraq had a heritage. There was a dome and a bunch of pointy arches and some elaborate scribbles in Arabic around the front door, which was three stories high. Scale, proportion, and ornamental detail were those of the Ritz-Carlton Tomb of Hammurabi or the Great Mosque in Disney World's Muslimland.

The palace was badly built. Shoddy rubble-wall construction was skimmed with a thin layer of concrete. Lines were scored in the cement, faking the seams of quarried stone. A missile had blown off the back of the palace, exposing its crawl spaces and utility rooms. The PVC plumbing and low-grade electrical wiring looked like things strewn around by a trailer-park tornado.

Inside, materials were marble, alabaster, mahogany, teak, and mother-of-pearl, elaborately handcrafted by badly skilled workmen. The main reception room was four floors high. A crystal chandelier hung down past two tiers of balconies. I paced off the shadow it cast on the floor. The chandelier was the size of a two-car garage. If a reason to invade Iraq was wanted, felony interior decorating would have done. Imagine Liberace as an inner-city high school basketball star who'd just signed an NBA contract and converted to Islam.

Returning to the airport from the palace, Major Bob and I saw civilians being searched at one of the checkpoints. A village that housed Iraqi airport workers was inside the airport security perimeter. Some of the villagers had fled during the war. Now they were coming back. But they had to be frisked first.

For propriety's sake, the women were asked to frisk themselves. They patted their chadors, or their jeans and T-shirts, with both hands from ankles to shoulders, maintaining a neutrality of expression that was admirable in a forced Macarena.

Najah Raheem, age fifty-one, had been hired by the Army to interpret at the checkpoint for three dollars a day.

"What did you do before the war?" Major Bob asked him.

"I was an air traffic controller."

"I'm probably living in your office," Major Bob said.

Najah suggested that we go to the village, called "the French Quarter" because it was built originally for the airport's French construction crews. "They will be eager to talk to you in the French Quarter," Najah said.

"They" was a formidable woman in black who had several of what seemed to be the village elders meekly in tow and any number of small boys and girls peering from behind her cloaks. "Three hundred families!" she said. "Many big families. Smallest families have five children. Ten days—no water, no electricity, no food, no cars."

One of the elders was brought forward to say, "The water main is broken" and "There are no wells."

"Is *this* the new Iraq?" the formidable woman said. "No schools. All night it is dark. We need *one* generator. There is no money. No doctor." She pointed to an old man. He had sores on his feet. He displayed them. "No insulin," the woman said.

Major Bob wanted to know if there had been any loot-ing or threats of violence in the village. "Are you safe?" he asked.

"Safe?" she replied. "Too safe! Ignore safe!"

Major Bob went to the Army Engineers. "We've got a little hearts-and-minds situation in our own backyard," he said. The officer on duty looked harried. The engineers knew about the problems in the French Quarter, but the French Quarter was hooked into the airport, and they hadn't been able to get the airport's main power and water systems work-ing. Anyway, orders would have to come from above.

"Which means a written report," Major Bob said, eye-ing me. Major Bob is an infantry officer by training and in-clination. But the Army thinks about its field officers what Harvard MBAs think about themselves: they can run any-thing. "I get to rotate out of public affairs next year," said Major Bob.

The most tendentious journalists don't write to accom-plish much except getting read. The most meticulous fact-checking departments don't check actual knowledge. It's remarkable how much about pipelines and electrical grids one reporter can be ignorant of. The report was delivered, and it joined, electronically, a queue of complaints, demands, and emergency appeals.

I went into Baghdad, tagging along on military errands. The city looked more like the target of a trash collectors' strike than the target of shock and awe. There were burned-out military vehicles here and there, but garbage was everywhere. The destruction from the air attacks had been highly specific, though wholesale within its specificity. Uday Hussein's Olympic training facility and supposed personal headquarters was erased, the rubble too flat even for low hurdles. The surrounding walls were untouched. An Interior Ministry building was a ten-story cinder, like the readable ash from a sheet of burned newspaper. Damage caused by the armor attack on the city was noticeable because it was newer, crisper, and more clean-edged than the general deterioration of Baghdad.

The men in the streets were sullen, and they were enthusiastic, and they were both. They stood with their buddies, glaring at American soldiers, and then rushed up to those soldiers to try to sell them something or change money. The women in the streets looked put-upon and harassed. Keeping the kids from playing on the tanks was just one more damn thing. The little boys carried ballpoint pens and wanted to have their arms signed by the soldiers.

Broken glass and twisted window gates from looting were all over the sidewalks. Improvised stalls of tradesmen were all over the sidewalks, too. How much of the trade was in loot I couldn't tell. The citizens of Baghdad were selling a lot of cigarettes and two-liter bottles of Fanta orange soda to one another. They were busy, though not with brooms and mops. I did see one man washing his car, however.

And there was another man, standing by his car in a long line at a gas station, who hid his AK-47 under his *dishdashah* as we drove by. The sound of AK-47s being shot could be heard at a distance from wherever American troops happened to be. Some of the shooting was rhythmic, celebratory "happy fire." Some was not, and came in single shots or short, discordant bursts. The gunfire increased after sundown.

If Kuwait is Houston without Enron, Baghdad is Washington, D.C., without Pierre L'Enfant. Wide boulevards have been plopped down anywhere amid an absurdity of monuments and monumental buildings and monumentally bad taste. A photograph of the soccer stadium could convince tabloid readers of an alien invasion. To commemorate victory (of which there was none) in the Iran-Iraq war, Baghdad's parade ground has a pair of boxcar-size hands popping out of the ground, holding crossed swords in a pot metal arch seventy feet high. And there's an identical arch at the parade ground's other end, to commemorate victory some more. The arches were untouched by the recent conflict. They formed a moving testimony to the discipline, training, and self-restraint of the U.S. Army's tank gunners.

An American armored battalion had occupied another Baghdad monument, a hundred-foot-tall split onion dome with both dome halves covered inside and out in bright-blue glazed ceramic tile. "We call it 'the tits,'" said a sentry at the monument's gate.

"Do you know what that is?" asked a reproving captain in whose Humvee I was riding. "It's the tomb of the Iraqi Unknown Soldier."

"Yes, sir," a second sentry said. "You'll find the colonel somewhere over by the eggshells."

Actually, the Unknown Soldier memorial was back across the river, at the crossed-swords parade ground. The dome sections (which more closely resemble baboon butt cheeks) memorialize *known* Iraqi soldiers—the million or so killed in the war with Iran. Their names and military units are inscribed in profusion around the structure's base, and inside, glass cases are full of the soldiers' belongings. This "Martyrs' Monument" is dedicated to ordinary Iraqis, although, according to the armored battalion's colonel, the only people allowed to visit it under Saddam's rule were members of the

Baath Party. One section of the interior was reserved solely for Saddam and his immediate family.

Saddam's family, or their moral ilk, had been using the Martyrs' Monument as a chop shop for stolen automobiles. An Iraqi carpenter hired to repair the car-thief damage was scared to go into the forbidden Saddam zone.

The looting of antiquities from the Iraq National Museum was not a good example of America's failure to protect Iraq's heritage. Dug in on the museum's grounds were squadrons of paramilitary *fedayeen*—not a part of Iraq's heritage that needed preserving. And do you shoot looters? A man running down the street with a two-hundred-pound head of Nebuchadnezzar in his arms can't hurt you. If you shoot someone who's got a Winged Lion of Assyria, he'll turn out to be a museum curator taking it home for safekeeping—or it will be a plastic Winged Lion of Assyria lawn ornament.

American tanks were guarding the National Museum with horse-gone, barn-door-closed acuity. I asked a tank crew, "Do you shoot looters?"

"Our operational orders are supposed to be secret," one crew member said.

"No," said another.

The looting of antiquities was not a good example of much of anything, considering where the objects in museums come from in the first place. Also, many of the most valuable archaeological treasures were hidden by the museum's staff. Others were trickling back to the museum. The Sumerian Sacred Vase of Warka was restituted by its thieves in June. According to *USA Today,* "The men returned the vase because they realized its importance to Iraq's heritage, officials said."

The official in charge the day I was at the museum, the director of research, Dr. Donny George, said, "Starting from yesterday we've stopped talking to the media." Television camera crews, news photographers, and other journalists had swept through the museum, grabbing images of pillage and snatching quotes from the staff.

One staff member sat atop what archaeologists call—or will call in a thousand years—a midden pile. The museum's lobby was heaped with crumpled records, letters, bills, and receipts. File cabinets had been pulled into the open space and their locks had been shot open. The locks had been shot open even on some newly delivered file cabinets, empty and still in their shipping wrappers. The staffer, an older man, smoothed pieces of paper. If it was an important piece of paper, he put it in a folder and sighed. If it wasn't, he threw it away and cursed. Every now and then a janitor would shove the discarded papers back into the unsorted pile. The rest of the museum staff sat around.

I'd come to the museum with soldiers from a Civil Affairs battalion. They were reservists with nonmilitary skills—firemen, policemen, engineers. One sergeant was getting his Ph.D. in sociology. With aid agencies yet to arrive, Civil Affairs had the job of fixing everything in Iraq that didn't need to be killed, although Civil Affairs had guns, too. Dr. George gave the soldiers a tour of the museum, and, uninvited, I went with them.

The galleries were a crime scene, but the parts of the museum that weren't open to the public were the scene of something else. Windows were broken. Furniture was smashed. Copiers, coffeemakers, typewriters, and telephones had been thrown around the rooms, and bullets had been fired into ceilings and walls. Bookshelves had been pulled over, and books and publications had been ripped and tossed. Archive photos were torn. Microfilm was unspooled and festooned like the remains of a ticker-tape parade in negative.

Rows of ancient pots had been staved in. Drawers' worth of carefully cataloged scholarly fragments had been further fragmentized. "Be careful," Dr. George said, "because you might be stepping on antiquities." Thousands-of-years-old crunches sounded under our feet.

The restoration studio was ruined. Tools were bent and broken. This wasn't looting. A gold Lyre of Ur had been stripped of its gold leaf; the lyre itself was on the floor. "Vandalism" was not the word. The Vandals controlled the Mediterranean with their sea power and forced the Roman emperor Valentinian III to make peace. They must have had brains. The people who did this to the National Museum were brainless enough to have gone to college with me. I remember just such a scene visited upon a persnickety landlord of off-campus housing. But I don't think the worst of my keg buddies would have trashed America's heritage. The looted Sumerians themselves, back from the dead and drunk as the lords they were, couldn't get this worked up at a museum.

One of the broken statues looked kind of Greek. "Hellenistic period," I said, in a lucky guess, to Dr. George. He smiled at me and began answering my media queries before I'd had a chance to make any.

"There were three groups of looters," Dr. George said. "First there were the experts." He explained that they had come equipped with glass cutters and battery-operated saws with stone-cutting blades. They knew what they were after and didn't take replicas or objects that had been over-restored. "Then there were the opportunists." He said that they took whatever they could and did most of the damage. "But then there is a third group—I don't know who they are. I don't understand. They are determined to burn all the libraries and archives in Baghdad, in all the colleges, at Baghdad University. They burned the central library. They burned all the postgraduate studies at the colleges. They burned the library here at the museum—just the library, not the other parts."

While I was interviewing Dr. George, curators from another museum arrived. This was the Museum of Modern Art, formerly known as the Saddam Hussein Museum of Modern Art, now renamed (for the moment, at least), as were the Saddam International Airport, the Saddam City housing project, the Saddam Hospital, and so on. It takes a certain kind of name to name everything after yourself. "P.J." wouldn't do: Pajama International Airport, Pajama City, Museum of Modern Pajamas.

The Museum of Modern Art had been looted, too. "Three or four hours ago we were chasing the looters," one of the curators said. But the staff had managed to get most of the museum's collection locked in the basement. Now, however, Baghdad's sewage system was backing up. Sewage was flooding into the museum cellar, and Iraq's entire collection of modern art was in peril.

The curators appealed to the Civil Affairs soldiers. "We need trucks," one of the curators said, "to bring the paintings here, where they will be guarded." The men from the Museum of Modern Art said it was America's responsibility. They said it was America's duty. They didn't say it was America's fault. But they were thinking it. And I was thinking that among the things America *didn't* bomb in Baghdad were the sewer outlets into the Tigris.

Major Bob woke me up the next morning. "The Civil Affairs guys scrounged a truck," he said. "We're going to save the modern art of Iraq."

It was a hundred degrees by ten A.M. Iraq's works of modern art tend to the large, also the numerous. We moved them from the mucky basement to the dusty truck as carefully as we could. Seeing a piece from a distance, Major Bob would say, "Now, that's a really bad Chagall"—but it would turn out to be painted in Chagall's extremely late period, when he was dead, and would be signed by someone local. "Well," Major Bob said, "it's their heritage, not ours."

The museum building had been rubbished. A couple of modern sculptures, too big to be hidden, were looking edgy and brutalist and, frankly, improved by the vandalism. Broken glass and shredded exhibit posters covered the entranceway. A young man in a disco haircut, sharply creased pants, and expensive shoes came to the gate. "Can I get into the museum?" he asked.

The sergeant who was getting his Ph.D. in sociology said, "It's very closed."

We dropped a truckload of art at the National Museum, half a mile away. I stayed behind to talk to Donny George.

Returning on foot, I got lost. Baghdad was, again, like Washington: I didn't have to wander far from the edifices to get into a slum. But rather than leaving the poor to the vagaries of outdated housing stock, the Iraqis had built their slums new. The two-story hovels, with one window apiece, were made of cement blocks left unpainted. There were tiny stores along the street. The shelves were vacant. People were loitering. I heard "Hello, American" several times from kids. I got "Welcome, please" from a couple proprietors of empty stores. There were a few hard stares from young men, who muttered after I'd passed. There were a few fewer wan smiles from old people.

I was in a flak vest that Major Bob insisted I wear for a visit to Baghdad, and my clothes were khaki from dirt. But I was too old to be a soldier, and I didn't have a television camera, so I couldn't be a journalist. I don't know how I appeared to the Iraqis. Mostly I didn't. I was invisible to the majority of people. Seventeen years before, in Belfast, British troops had had this invisibility. Squadrons in battle gear would patrol the Republican stronghold of Divis Flats, and to the Irish they weren't there. The British have ended up spending nine centuries in Ireland.

I found my way back to the Museum of Modern Art. A television crew from Bahrain had arrived. The soldiers were being interviewed about the importance of Iraq's cultural heritage. An eight-foot canvas depicting an innocent Iraqi being smothered by an American flag and pecked by a bald eagle had just been pulled from the cellar. The TV reporter, Saad al-Hasani, was also an assistant professor of English at the University of Baghdad. I asked him if he knew anything about the "third group" of looters who Dr. George had said were burning libraries.

Professor al-Hasani had gone to stay with relatives in the country during the war. His apartment in Baghdad had been looted. He'd expected that. But someone had carried all his books down to the apartment building's yard and burned them.

"I teach modern theater," he said. "My specialty is Samuel Beckett and the theater of the absurd. I'd always had trouble explaining Beckett to my students. They didn't comprehend the theater of the absurd. Then, after the war in 1991, my students suddenly were starting to understand *Waiting for Godot.* I could tell by the questions they asked in class, by their essays. It was if they were anticipating something. There was a situation in the air. A student came up to me and said, 'This is just like *Waiting for Godot.* Nobody comes. Nobody goes. It's awful. *Nothing to be done.*'"

I told Professor al-Hasani about the book cover in the airport administration-building locker. Would air traffic controllers and aeronautical engineers be reading *Godot,* too?

"Of course," he said.

That evening at the airport a major and a lieutenant colonel from the Civil Affairs battalion drove the truck around scrounging material to build a latrine. The major was a mechanical engineer. The colonel was an electrical engineer. They argued as if they were married.

"We can build a lighter frame if we stress the plywood in monocoque construction."

"Fuck lightness—compression equals strength."

I pounded nails, rather crookedly. It was an innovative outhouse. Cut-down fifty-five-gallon oil drums were set on airport luggage trolleys so that waste cans could be rolled in under the seats.

"You have seen the backside of war," the electrical engineer said.

*   *   *

In the morning Major Bob woke me again. "We're going to the French Quarter with Civil Affairs," he said. I thought proudly about the written report—for a few minutes. Then the Civil Affairs batallion commander said, "Some Special Forces guys were patrolling through there. They told us it was a mess. We're only supposed to do an assessment, but we've scrounged some tools, and we were scrounging around in the terminal and found a bunch of antibiotics and medical supplies the Iraqis had hidden."

We were greeted by the village elder who'd said the water main was broken. Without the formidable woman, he was more talkative. He said the American attack on the airport came through the middle of the French Quarter. The area had been defended by Iraqi secret police, but not very well, to judge by the slight shell and bullet damage. The village elder said he'd been a fire chief for thirty years. The French Quarter was not a cap to his career. After a secret-police vehicle was hit by an American rocket, a house caught fire, and the entire block burned down. Ten families were left homeless, but fortunately they were homeless already, having fled from the war.

Tarik al-Wasty, a carpenter and pipe fitter at the airport, had spent the five days of the bombing and assault lying on the floor of his house with his wife and ten children. He showed me a hole where a tank round had come into his garden, and offered me tea. His two-year-old son was still terrified, would sleep only if curled beneath his father, and was coughing continually. A medical corpsman brought some drugs from the Iraqi cache. The corpsmen tried to explain to Tarik, whose English was not good, that steam could be used to help clear the child's chest. Getting a blank stare, the corpsman attempted charades and was prevented from persuading Tarik to boil his toddler in a pot by the family's nine-year-old son, whose English was excellent.

The electrical-engineer lieutenant colonel had discovered fellow electrical engineers among the French Quarter residents. They were probing the innards of a transformer. The mechanical-engineer major had found additional engineers. They were inspecting the water main, which had been crushed by a tank. "I think I know where there's a big piece of pipe I can scrounge," the mechanical engineer said.

Major Bob and I looked at the school. It was the one public building I saw in Iraq that hadn't been looted. There were only a few bullet holes in the walls. The school was decorated with murals of Smurfs and Mickey Mouse drawn, it looked like, by the painter of the Chagalls at the Museum of Modern Art.

The fire chief and some of his friends gave us a tour of the village. The houses were prefab, semidetached, and looked like modest European vacation cottages but with bomb shelters in their yards. Recreation facilities had been provided for the previous construction-worker tenants—a picnic area, a swimming pool, tennis and volleyball courts. The nets were gone. The poles were bent double. The swimming pool was half-filled with chunks of concrete. The picnic area was layered in trash. The fire chief said something about "repairs forbidden" and that the French Quarter had fallen out of favor with Saddam Hussein. If appearances were any indication, so had the rest of Iraq.

"Having looked at the Mideast," Major Bob said, "I realize how the Arabs came up with the concept of zero."

Will a strong Iraq emerge from the chaos? Let's hope not. But will the Iraqi people become part of the modern, free, and prosperous world? That's possible, though I have only one piece of anecdotal evidence to go by. I was riding through Baghdad in the last truck of an Army convoy, with a unit that will go unidentified because drinking was a punishable offense for U.S. troops in Iraq. We spotted a man selling beer on the street. "I'd better stop," said the sergeant who was driving, "and check my windshield-wiper fluid level or something."

I jumped out of the truck. "Let me do this," I said. "I've been coming to the Middle East for twenty years. I *know* how to *haggle*."

"How much for the whole case?" I asked the vendor in pidgin and gesture.

"Twenty bucks," he said in English.

Twenty dollars was a fortune in Baghdad at that moment. Also, I didn't have twenty dollars. I had a ten and a bunch of Kuwaiti dinars. The vendor looked askance at the dinars. The soldiers weren't carrying much money, either. They came up with another six dollars among them.

I dickered with the beer merchant. He bargained. I chiseled. We bandied. A crowd gathered to watch. Some teenage Iraqi boys, seeing an Asian-American soldier in the truck, hollered, "*Thigh Cone Do!*" and exhibited awkward kicks.

The seller of beer and I concluded a deal of considerable financial complexity involving U.S. dollars and Kuwaiti dinars, with change in Iraqi dinars at an exchange rate determined by consensus among the purchase's spectators.

Back in the truck, as we tried to catch up with our convoy, I did the math. I had bargained my way from $20 to a final price of $24.50. And the beer turned out to be nonalcoholic. Baghdad will be Houston *with* Enron.

10

POSTSCRIPT: IWO JIMA

AND THE END OF

MODERN WARFARE

July 2003

As a memorial to the astonishing war-slaughter of the modern age, I propose the island of Iwo Jima—for its ugliness, its uselessness, and its remoteness from all things of concern to the postmodern era.

Iwo Jima can be visited only with military permission and, usually, only by military transport. A comfortless C-130 Hercules propeller craft flies from Okinawa over seven hundred miles of blank Pacific, moving as slowly as the planes of Iwo's battle days. The island is five miles long, running northeast from a neck of sand at the base of the partly collapsed Mount Suribachi volcanic cone and spreading to a width of two and a half miles in the shape of a paint spill, with Mount Suribachi (really a 550-foot hill) as the can of

paint. The colors are gray, gray-green, brown, and black—
the hues of camouflage. From the air Iwo Jima looks as small
as it is, a reminder of the insignificance of the great tactical
objectives of war. The landscape at Ypres is banal. The beaches
at Normandy are not as nice as those on Cape Cod. From the
top of Cemetery Ridge at Gettysburg the prospect is less awe-
inspiring than the view from many interstate rest stops. And
Iwo Jima protrudes unimpressively from an oceanic reminder
of the insignificance of everything.

I went to Iwo Jima with a director and a cameraman. We
were working on a one-hour cable television documentary
about the battle. Between February 19 and March 26, 1945,
6,821 Americans and about 20,000 Japanese were killed in
the fight for the island. How could a one-hour anything—
prayer, symphony, let alone cable television documentary—
do justice to that? The director, the cameraman, and I had
worried about it the night before in an Okinawa bar. We
decided that 26,821 men would have told us to knock off
the chickenshit worrying and drink.

The three of us were guests on a trip that is offered pe-
riodically to young enlisted Marines, in recognition of exem-
plary performance and attitude. The journey is spoken of as
a "morale booster." It was summer. Iwo Jima is almost on the
Tropic of Cancer, parboiled by the North Equatorial Current.
In the sun its charcoal briquette rocks become a hibachi. The
temperature remained over a hundred degrees at midnight.
The humidity was 100 percent. When there was wind, it was
an eructation. The volcanic vents on Iwo Jima are still active.
The name means "Sulfur Island" in Japanese. The Marines
were not allowed to smoke or swim or explore on their own.
They slept on the ground. Reveille was at five A.M. They were
led on hikes all day, covering the island's 8.5 square miles. I

was never in the military, but if this is what boosts morale, I want nothing to do with what causes morale to deteriorate.

However, young men and women do not join the Marines to get comfortable. And going to Iwo Jima is a way for new Marines to imbue themselves with the spirit of the Corps. The battle for the island was fought by the largest force of Marines that had ever been assembled. The casualties were shocking. More than a third of the nearly seventy-five thousand Marines who landed on Iwo Jima were killed or wounded. The bravery, too, was shocking. Of the 353 Congressional Medals of Honor awarded during World War II, twenty-seven were given for heroism on Iwo Jima, thirteen posthumously.

"Iwo" became a byword for fighting while it was still being fought. The U.S. military had hoped the island could be taken in two weeks. The battle lasted thirty-six days. Japanese resistance was expected to be stubborn. It was ferocious. Only 1,083 of the approximately 21,000 Japanese defenders surrendered or were taken prisoner. The landing on Iwo Jima occurred as the war in Europe was ending. The Allies were on the Rhine. Warsaw had fallen. Attention turned to the Pacific theater. The Secretary of the Navy himself, James V. Forrestal, was on the beach at Iwo Jima on "D-day plus four." When Secretary Forrestal saw the flag-raising on Mount Suribachi, he said, "This means a Marine Corps for the next five hundred years."

And there is that flag-raising. The Associated Press photographer Abe Rosenthal's shot is the best-known image of combat in World War II—perhaps the best-known image of combat in history. The word "icon," blunted with use, can be applied precisely to the picture of the flag-raising on Mount Suribachi. Rendered in bronze at the Marine Corps War Memorial, with men thirty-two feet tall, the flag-raising is more impressive than the mountain where it happened.

To the young—very young—Marines who were looking at that mountain when I was there, the flag-raising must seem to have happened a full Secretary Forrestal five-hundred-years ago. For someone born in 1984, the war between Japan and the United States is almost as long past as the war between Japan and Czarist Russia is for me. During that protracted meander of chronology, Iwo Jima acquired a slight, untoward comic tinge. There were numerous parodic representations of the monument, the photo, the pose. There were Johnny Carson's "Mount Suribachi" tag lines. There was a period of years when every drunk of a certain age who'd ever been a Marine claimed to have fought at Iwo, my uncle Mike included. (Uncle Mike's World War II Marine Corps stint was spent in a stateside hospital with an infected toe.) John Wayne didn't fight there, either, but he gave a clumsy imitation of doing so in *Sands of Iwo Jima*. When televisions became common, that movie appeared on them constantly. The photograph itself did not show the first American flag atop Suribachi but, rather, its replacement with a second, larger Stars and Stripes. It is an image of combat in which no combat is involved. One or two too many men are trying to shove an iron pipe into a pile of rocks. And the flag-raising was not a signal of victory. It happened on the fifth day of the invasion, when most of the fighting and dying were yet to come.

The Marines of 2003 woke up on their first morning on Iwo Jima and hiked four miles from their campground to the top of Suribachi. They did it so quickly that they were there for sunrise, at 5:45. They hung their dog tags at Suribachi's peak, on a bas-relief of the flag-raising mounted on a granite plinth. The monument is decorated with hundreds of dog tags, many bearing dates of birth more recent than my last dentist appointment. But if there was anything that struck the young Marines as antique or absurd about this battlefield, they didn't show it. Some of them will be sent to deal with the antique absurdities of Afghanistan and Iraq.

The director, the cameraman, and I—antiques in our forties and fifties—proceeded on our own absurd errand. Bearing camera, tripod, battery packs, tapes, and so forth, we trudged through a satire of tropical paradise. The beaches were black, not white. The sea looked like agitated dishwater. The sky was cloudless, but dull with heat haze. Palm trees did not sway, nor did bougainvillea flower in the botanically anonymous uninterrupted scrub. The weather didn't warm the blood, it broiled the bald spot and baked the feet. In place of grass shacks and tiki huts were the ruins of Japanese pill-boxes and gun emplacements.

The three of us carried our stuff across the island and up Suribachi and down. We didn't faint in the heat or get too dizzy and sick. Iwo Jima is not a place, we complained to one another, where you feel you're allowed to complain. We went out into the deep, steep-pitched sucking sand of the D-day landing beaches. Thirty thousand men were put ashore that morning in a space hardly adequate for a UCLA panhellenic luau. Tanks, amphibious vehicles, and Marines themselves sank to immobility. On D-day, 2,420 Americans were killed or wounded.

Combat now is a less crowded affair and more dependent on sophisticated electronic equipment. We were lugging some. It didn't compare in heft to what a Marine carried on a World War II amphibious landing. In 1945 one man's weapons, ammunition, and gear might have weighed as much as 122 pounds. Killing is not as physical as it once was. It's time for young, hopeful people to be relieved of fighting duties. War should be fought by the middle-aged men who, anyway, decide that war should be fought. We don't have our whole lives in front of us. We're already staring down the barrel of heart disease and SEC investigations. Being wrenched from home, family, and job wouldn't be that wrenching for many of us. We wouldn't need these morale-boosting trips.

The irony of unarmed old guys didn't appear to register on the young Marines. They had brought pocketsful of small Ziploc bags and were filling these with sands of Iwo Jima.

Perhaps that movie deserves another, unironic look. *Sands of Iwo Jima*, released in 1949, doesn't have much to do with the battle, although the final scenes are set on Iwo and incorporate harrowing footage shot by Marine combat cameramen. The movie's real subject is a change in America, a nationwide 150-million-person shift in values. John Wayne, a Marine sergeant, is tough as nails. John Agar, a private in Wayne's platoon, is sensitive and has been to college. They clash. "I want my son to be intelligent, not tough," Agar tells Wayne, who is shown to be pretty damn sensitive himself and more intelligent than you'd think. Then Wayne gets shot, and Agar realizes that sometimes the sensitive, intelligent thing to do is to be tough as nails. *Sands of Iwo Jima* thus traces U.S. foreign policy from Teddy Roosevelt's Big Stick through Woodrow Wilson's Fourteen Points to George Bush's Whatever-It-Turns-Out-to-Be.

It's tempting to believe that the Japanese defenders of Iwo Jima weren't as sensitive as Americans. The Japanese fought for the island mostly from underground, hiding in sixteen miles of tunnels and caves. They died in there from flamethrower attacks, satchel charge explosions, and suffocation. Many Japanese dead remain in these catacombs. Narrow, scary orifices of the tunnel system open all over the island. Visiting relatives have placed small altars by the holes. Offerings of cigarettes and sake sit beside incense burners. Broken and rusted weapons are arranged gracefully. It's just not possible for a sensitive American peering into the dreadful apertures to think that every person inside was as miserable and frightened as I would have been.

In fact, the Japanese military men on Iwo Jima, or at least the officers, were arguably more sensitive—and more intelligent—than their American counterparts. The island's commander, Lieutenant General Tadamichi Kuribayashi, was an accomplished artist. He was fluent in English. He spent several years as a military attaché in the United States and Canada, writing letters home to his wife and child, the pages filled with humorous cartoons. And he openly opposed going to war with America. The head of naval forces, Rear Admiral Toshinosuke Ichimaru, wrote poetry in Japanese and classical Chinese and was famous for his calligraphy. Lieutenant Colonel Takeichi Nishi was sensitive to opportunities for fun. He was a baron, of the gossip-column-boldface variety, who won a gold medal in horse-jumping in the 1932 Los Angeles Olympics. He partied in Hollywood, had affairs with actresses, and knew Spencer Tracy. All three officers fought to the death.

Across the northern fan of Iwo Jima a volcanic plateau is half eroded into disorderly hills. Mostly their names are nothing but their heights in feet: Hill 382, Hill 362A, and so on. Every hill caused hundreds of people to die; so did every ravine between them. Any clump of rocks providing cover was a source of death, as were all open spaces providing none. Almost five men to an acre were killed for this island, a corpse in each subdivision house lot. On D-day Lieutenant Colonel Charles E. Shepard, Jr., the commander of the Third Battalion, Twenty-eighth Marine Regiment, told his men that their objective was "to secure this lousy piece of real estate so we can get the hell off it." William Manchester, in his memoir of the Pacific war, *Goodbye, Darkness*, described Iwo Jima as "an ugly, smelly glob of cold lava squatting in a surly ocean."

By coincidence, just a month earlier, I'd been looking at other smelly globs on the far side of the same surly ocean, in the equally isolated Galapagos Islands. My fellow tourists and I *oooh*ed at the black sands, *aaah*ed at the sulfurous volcano vents, and told one another how beautiful the sunset was behind mounts of exactly Suribachi's shape. Iwo Jima does not have the strange life-forms found in the Galapagos. But what form of life could be stranger than that which was lived on Iwo Jima from February 19 to March 26, 1945? The Galapagos Islands are internationally protected, to preserve the history of biological evolution. On Iwo Jima the history of moral evolution is preserved. The litter of battle is lying where it was dropped. A seven-story Japanese fortification inside Mount Suribachi has never been reentered.

After Iwo Jima a few more big World War II battles took place, notably in Berlin and on Okinawa. But it wasn't long before sensitive, intelligent nations evolved beyond such things—even if Hiroshima, one of those cataclysmic events common to evolutionary history, was required to spark the progress. Since then military hordes swarming in all-out attack and military masses falling in desperate defense have been rare. When they do happen, evolutionary throwbacks are involved—Kim Il Sung, the Ayatollah Khomeini, Saddam Hussein.

People have not gotten better, of course—just more sensitive and, maybe, intelligent. One of the things they are intelligent about is strategy. Iwo Jima is 660 miles from Tokyo. At the beginning of 1945 Americans had Pacific air bases that were within range of the Japanese mainland for bombers but not for fighter escorts. If the Americans could take Iwo Jima, B-29s would fly over Tokyo fully protected. If the Japanese could keep Iwo Jima, B-29s would not. Today ninety-six thousand soldiers aren't thrown into one such small space on a map. There are so many other kinds of space to fight over—outer space, cyberspace, the space between most people's ears.

We gave Iwo Jima back to Japan in 1968. It is now, as it was in February 1945, a Japanese military base. At sunset when I was there, the Japanese national anthem was played over loudspeakers near the Marine campground. Every U.S. Marine turned toward the Japanese flag, stood at attention, and saluted. A Marine sergeant said under his breath, "My grandfather would be rolling over in his grave if he saw this."

Neither his grandfather nor any other American is rolling over in his grave on Iwo Jima. The American dead were disinterred in the 1960s and returned to American soil. Their ghosts don't haunt the Iwo Jima battlefield. Nor do the ghosts of the Japanese. I don't believe in ghosts, but I'm Irish enough to be able to tell when none are around. The island is grim. Thoughts of its history are frightening. But Iwo Jima isn't spooky. I found the same notion in James Michener's *Tales of the South Pacific*. At the end of the book the narrator visits a military cemetery. He encounters a black sailor who has volunteered for caretaker duty.

"Isn't it strange," I asked, "for colored men to like work in a cemetery?"

My guide laughed gently and easily. "Yes! Yes! I know jes' what yo'-all means," he said. "All dem jokes about ghos's and cullud men. But what yo'-all doan' see," he added quietly, "is dat dey ain' no ghos's up here! . . . dey is only heros."

Pardon, for the sake of the thought, Michener's insensitive language. He was a pre-postmodern man. And so was General Kuribayashi. In his last message to Imperial General Headquarters he said, "Even as a ghost, I wish to be a vanguard of future Japanese operations." If so, he's haunting a Toyota factory.

General Kuribayashi sent his message from a cave in a ravine at the northwest corner of Iwo Jima, an area that the Americans called Bloody Gorge. The Marines of 1945 were plagued by the manifold bolt-holes, peek holes, and gun ports concealed in the narrow jumble of rock and brush.

I went to Kuribayashi's final redoubt with a Marine sergeant major and his Japanese counterpart. The sergeants major are friends. They are authorities on the history of Iwo Jima. Together they gave lectures to the young Marines and guided the hikes around the island.

I couldn't see the entrance to Kuribayashi's cave—even though his descendants had marked it with a statue of a Shinto goddess. The sergeants, on their bellies, led me inside. Kuribayashi was a wide man, five feet nine and two hundred pounds. Getting him into his headquarters must have been like opening wine when the corkscrew is lost. Thirty feet down, the roof, walls, and floor of the cave flared like a panic attack. We stood in a large, hot, stinking chamber with dead men's belongings all over the ground.

By early March Kuribayashi had only fifteen hundred men. They were all in one square mile around Bloody Gorge. Tens of thousands of Marines were on the island. The American Pacific command declared Iwo Jima "secure" on March 14. Yet the fighting continued for twelve more days. In the "mopping up" on Iwo Jima, 1,071 Marines were killed. As of my visit to Iwo that was fewer Americans than had died in the conquest and occupation of Iraq, with its 167,000 square miles of territory and its army of half a million men.

We're coming to the end of the long, dark modern age. Slaughters of unnumbered human beings continue, but not among people who knew Spencer Tracy. Warfare persists, but the scale of battle is returning to something that the author of the *Iliad* would recognize. Maybe someday each combat casualty will rate the kind of mourning that Achilles did for Patroclus, except on television, and the saga of every Jessica Lynch will be an *Odyssey* or, anyway, a cover of *People*. There never will be peace, but we can have wars where, when we talk about our soldiers, we say, "Dey is only heros."

P. J. O'ROURKE

Holidays in Hell

PICADOR

In *Holidays in Hell* America's funniest writer takes on the role of tour guide with hilarious results. In this darkly satirical take on the travel-writing genre, O'Rourke reports from trouble spots around the world; 'A Ramble through Lebanon' and 'Christmas in El Salvador' may sound unpromising, but when subjected to O'Rourke's blackly comic treatment they become gloriously entertaining inversions of the standard travelogue. The perfect antidote to political correctness, *Holidays in Hell* is also a clear-eyed look at humanity, or man's lack of it, around the world.

P. J. O'ROURKE

GIVE WAR A CHANCE

PICADOR

Opening with an introduction entitled 'Hunting the Virtuous' – 'and How to Clean and Skin Them', the author provides his own comments on the people, places and events behind the newspaper headlines, before launching into an account of the Gulf War. Beginning with a concise history of the Middle East, he delivers a day-to-day chronicle of the tedium of waiting for war in the Saudi desert, signing off with an eyewitness account of the victory march into Kuwait city.

P. J. O'ROURKE

EAT THE RICH

PICADOR

A conservative, prosperous American journalist gadding around the world laughing at all the ways less successful nations screw up their economy – this might not sound like the recipe for a great read, unless you're Rush Limbaugh, but if that journalist is P.J. O'Rourke you can be sure that you'll enjoy the ride even if you don't agree with the politics. Although *Eat the Rich* is subtitled *A Treatise on Economics*, O'Rourke spends relatively few pages tackling the complexities of monetary theory. He's much happier when flying from Sweden to Hong Kong, then on to Tanzania and Moscow, gleefully recording every economic goof he can find. When he visits post-Soviet Russia and finds a country that is as messed up by capitalism as it was by communism, O'Rourke mixes jokes about black-market shoes with disturbing insights into a nation on the verge of collapse. P.J. O'Rourke is more than a humorist, he's an experienced international journalist with a lot of frequent-flyer miles and this gives even his funniest riffs on the world's problems a startling ring of truth.

P. J. O'ROURKE

The CEO of the Sofa

PICADOR

Another perspicacious look at the Byzantine nature of the secrets of business success, with hilarious close-ups of some of O'Rourke's favourite subjects. This confirms his unassailable position as 'America's greatest prose comedian' (*Sunday Times*). Bestselling humorist O'Rourke introduces readers to his assistant, friends, family and smart-aleck babysitter, as he reflects on such topics as cell phones, Christmas catalogues, Instant Messaging, toddlers, TV and how the 'Gettysburg Address' would have turned out if written on an iMac. He reviews Hillary Clinton, and he observes youth culture, including current celebs, Britney, Moby and Eminem. This is a witty wide-angled world view, from O'Rourke's own living room.

ANTHONY LANE

Nobody's Perfect

PICADOR

Reviewer and critic with the *New Yorker* for over ten years, Anthony Lane is infamous for his acerbic wit and wry observations. Never afraid of controversy, he writes with a refreshing frankness – 'What is the point of Demi Moore?' – about everything from Shakespeare to *The Sound of Music*, Oscar night to Alfred Hitchcock. Highbrow culture, bestselling books, blockbusting films, fashion, art, author profiles, poetry: Lane writes about it all with a passion that makes for a perfect read.

'Anthony Lane must be the fizziest critic around. Each paragraph tickles the nose like a flute of champagne. His ebulliently active mind and wonderfully cluttered memory work to make us laugh aloud while he slips in the dirk, its edges painlessly keen, of urbane, humane opinion'
John Updike

'Anthony Lane has energy, wit, taste and learning'
Martin Amis

OTHER BOOKS
AVAILABLE FROM PAN MACMILLAN

P. J. O'ROURKE
HOLIDAYS IN HELL	0 330 30683 9	£7.99
GIVE WAR A CHANCE	0 330 32536 1	£6.99
EAT THE RICH	0 330 35328 4	£6.99
THE CEO OF THE SOFA	0 330 49143 6	£7.99

ANTHONY LANE
NOBODY'S PERFECT	0 330 49183 0	£9.99

MARK LAWSON
ENOUGH IS ENOUGH OR
THE EMERGENCY GOVERNMENT	0 330 43803 4	£16.99

All Pan Macmillan titles can be ordered from our website,
www.panmacmillan.com, or from your local bookshop
and are also available by post from:

Bookpost, PO Box 29, Douglas, Isle of Man IM99 1BQ
Credit cards accepted. For details:
Telephone: +44 (0)1624 677237
Fax: +44 (0)1624 670923
E-mail: bookshop@enterprise.net
www.bookpost.co.uk

Free postage and packing in the United Kingdom

Prices shown above were correct at the time of going to press.
Pan Macmillan reserve the right to show new retail prices on covers
which may differ from those previously advertised in the text
or elsewhere.